D0017488

Little Seed Publishing
Laguna Beach, CA

Pre-press Management by New Caledonian Press
Text Design: Angie Kimbro

Cover Design and Illustrations: K-Squared Designs, LLC, www.k2ds.com

Acknowledgement is made for permission to quote copyrighted materials.

Printed in the United States of America.

For information, contact Little Seed Publishing's operations office at Global Partnership: P.O. Box 894, Murray, KY 42071, or phone 270-753-5225 (CST).

Distributed by Global Partnership, LLC
P.O. Box 894
Murray, KY 42071

Library of Congress Cataloguing in Publication Data
Wake Up... Live the Life You Love: Wake Up Moments
ISBN-13: 978-1-933063-12-6

$14.95 USA $14.95 Canada

Other books by Steven E, and Lee Beard

Wake Up…Live the Life You Love:

…First Edition

…Second Edition

…Inspirational How-to Stories

…In Beauty

…Living on Purpose

…Finding Your Life's Passion

…Purpose, Passion, Abundance

…Finding Personal Freedom

…Seizing Your Success

…Giving Gratitude

…On the Enlightened Path

…In Spirit

…Finding Life's Passion

…Stories of Transformation

…A Search for Purpose

...Living in Abundance

...Living in Clarity

...The Power of Team

Wake Up…Shape Up…Live the Life You Love

Wake Up...
Live the Life You Love

Wake Up Moments

TABLE OF CONTENTS

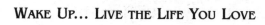

INTRODUCTION

Wake up!

Sure: we've all done that. We do it every morning. Then we go to work, take care of the regular list of business, come home late, wash, rinse, repeat.

But how many of us have really taken the time to reflect on what's happening in our lives? To sit back and analyze what's really going on, or focus on what we really want and where we are going? Sometimes we get stuck in a rut and we often fail to recognize those little chimes and tiny signs that are calling out to us, "Wake Up!"

This book is a compilation of stories about people who realized, sometimes over a long period, that they were getting their wake up call. They were being called to do something more with their lives, to get up, wake up and realize something important they had been missing. And, as Lee Beard says, "They finally stopped hitting the snooze button."

In the pages that follow, you will read how they focus on the moment in time when they found their purpose and awoke their passion. They focus on the mentors and guides who showed them the plan and brought them to the realizations and associations that led them to success. All those things, both little and great, made all the difference and changed their lives.

After reading this you may be able to identify some of the wake up calls you've had. Perhaps at first they weren't obvious; perhaps you were too busy to recognize them. Whatever the case we hope that maybe—just maybe—some of these stories will help you identify the wake up call you've been missing.

Don't miss your wake up call. Stop hitting the snooze button, get out of bed and get into a life you truly love!

Wake Up...
Live the Life You Love

Wake Up Moments

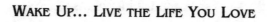

WHAT IS IN IT FOR YOU?

Lee Beard

It began when Steven E, the creator of the *Wake Up…Live the Life You Love* best-selling book series, shared his "wake up moment," which led us to start a documentary about the venture. That, in turn, has grown into a worldwide connection of people sharing the moment that started them moving along their various career paths.

As we have encouraged others to tell of their "wake up moment," we heard many wonderful stories. One of the joys has been interviewing celebrities before the Emmy Awards and the Oscars. In these interviews, we heard how David Krumholtz was encouraged by his teacher to go to open auditions in New York. Gary Anthony Williams shared his recollection about how he was put in an acting class in high school by a computer error. Ernie Hudson heard a voice telling him to "take the tube out" of his television, which prompted conversation with his wife, which turned their life around.

Television star Blair Underwood knew at the age of nine he loved playing make believe, but he also knew he had to go to college. The "wake up moment" came when he realized that he could go to college, study acting, be on television and make money. Liz Vassey, at nine years old, saw her sister in a play and told her mom that she wanted to try acting.

All of these amazing stories led these actors to pursue their passions and dreams. In turn, they found satisfaction, fame and security for their families. We hope that their stories encourage you to be bold and, like them, to start doing what you love today.

It may not be easy at first. You may find a mentor to teach and guide you, and point the way to a lifetime of happiness and fulfillment. To be sure, the one consistent thread in all these wonder stories is this: All the vision and guidance in the world will not carry you to the goal you seek. They may light the path, but the steps—one at a time—must be yours; your effort, your dedication and your commitment to the life you love.

The most important moment I can recall was when, at 12 years old, I accepted Jesus Christ as my personal Savior. I remember it as if it were yesterday. I thought at the time that it was the happiest moment of my life, and it has been the foundation of everything that has happened to me. I would like to say that I have always been faithful and true to my belief in God and Christ, but the truth is that God has been faithful to me and never let me stray too far from His love, guidance, provision and protection.

Get a solid foundation for your life, get the training from the very best people and give it a go! We hope these captured "moments" will inspire you. Perhaps they will prepare you to recognize the importance of a moment that might otherwise pass virtually unnoticed. Perhaps they will encourage you to act on the passion that comes to life during these remarkable incidents we call the "wake up moment."

We want you to share your story with us and, perhaps, with the whole world. If you wish, you may join us at: Wakeupmoment.com. Who knows? Perhaps yours is the moment that will ignite the flame to illuminate the paths of others.

Live happy, and love it all!

Lee Beard

THROWING OUT THE TUBE
Ernie Hudson

I graduated from high school, but not the same way or with the same sense of joy and accomplishment that many people share.

My grandmother raised me and I was told to get a high school education, which I did. However, she never said anything about my grades; I graduated with a D average. Then, to make the road to the future even bumpier, I got married at 18. My wife got pregnant right away, and suddenly, one day, it hit me: this was my life. I was working in a factory and I just felt trapped; I had no way out. I thought, "Maybe I'll go to college." But when I tried to get into college that D average came into play. I couldn't get accepted anywhere.

One night, I just prayed over the whole mess that my life had become. Finally, I drifted off into sleep. I woke up around three in the morning, and I heard a voice saying, "Go downstairs and take the tube out of the TV." You may not believe it, but I did just what I had been told. Of course, when I took the tube out of the TV, my wife thought it was broken. With no TV in the evening, we had to fall back on simple conversation.

For the first time in our married lives, we started to really talk to each other. I found out that my wife was a great reader; she had a deep interest in people and in the world around her, and had the same kind of aspirations that I held in my heart. Well, we just turned our lives around. She was in the ninth grade when we got married, but she went on to get her Ph.D. I finally got into college at Wayne State, followed by a scholarship to Yale, and then I attended the University of Minnesota. On stage or screen, I've been doing what I love to do ever since.

I can never forget that there was one moment when I just *knew* I had to make a change. It was a moment of knowing, "I know there's another way, and I'm not seeing it." Sometimes you just have to ask for help. My life

has never been—and never will be—the same. I literally woke up.
We watched so much TV those first months we were married; but I couldn't remember what we had watched the night before. Once we started to really communicate with each other we realized that we both had dreams—a vision of what we wanted to do and what we wanted to achieve in life. At that moment, we began to climb out of the hole we had put ourselves in.

What's your dream? Young people are often told to forget their dreams and prepare for a life of practicality. Acting or any career in theatre, they are told, is impractical. Well, if you really want to act, I say, "Do what you want to do." I talk to people every day who say they want to be an actor, but they only want to be in movies, be seen on TV, and be recognized as a celebrity. There is so much more to living a dream.

I discovered acting in college. College is a great place to really understand your craft. I was able to learn what acting is all about. It's not about becoming rich and famous, it's about learning a craft and being able to do it for a lifetime. I've been doing acting for 40 years, and that's what it's about. To really live the life you love and to live it with meaning, you may have to change your priorities and your goals. It's not about all the pretended glamour and celebrity status, because those things really don't matter at the end of the day.

I have four sons: my two younger boys are in college and my two older sons have graduated from college. They have gotten their advanced degrees. I am so happy for them because they have laid the foundation for living a good life; a decent life. No matter what your career path, the same warning holds true: if you are looking for the glamour, the fame, and the recognition, you are searching for an empty treasure chest. You are on the road to a very dead end.

So I would say you should lay out a strong foundation, because that foundation is what is going to carry you over the years. In spite of a few moments of possible glory, you don't really want to end up like so many friends I have known who are angry, bitter and disappointed because they

were unfavorably compared to somebody else or they didn't quite get what they thought they wanted.

Reality is this: find your craft, study and train. Follow your dream, but never forget: before you can follow a dream, you have to wake up.

Ernie Hudson

WHY WAIT FOR A SECOND CHANCE?

Laura Bank, Ph.D., PA-C

Julie, my wonderful nurse, looked like a ghost. She said, "Laura, I have to tell you something." Her tone was very serious. She continued, "I was Scott's hospice nurse." I think my heart stopped.

I studied Scott's medical chart to learn about his history before he came to see me as a patient for the first time. During our interaction, he filled me in on the details to answer my remaining questions. I was surprised that he seemed to downplay his journey until I realized it didn't matter to him anymore. He had been given a golden ticket for a second chance at life.

Scott Johnson, who has given me permission to share his story, was born with a rare genetic disease called cystic fibrosis. Cystic fibrosis affects the lungs and digestive system. It causes the body to produce thick mucus that clogs the lungs and prevents the pancreas from producing enzymes needed to digest food. The average life span for someone with this disease is about 37. There is no cure.

Scott was diagnosed with cystic fibrosis at two months old, when he was admitted to the hospital for pneumonia and a collapsed lung. Growing up, he was embarrassed about his constant medical needs and incessant coughing. His disease played a major role as he grew up because "people with cystic fibrosis don't think about their future."

When Scott was in his late 20s, he became very sick. An oxygen machine helped him breathe, and he was frequently admitted to the hospital for infections. He lost a tremendous amount of weight, dropping down to 95 pounds. Scott became sicker and was admitted to the hospital yet again. They told him he had about a week to live.

Hospice was called in to provide medical care and services to Scott and his family as his death drew near. The only thing that could save him was a double lung transplant. On his deathbed, Scott made a list of all of the things he wished he could do if he lived. The first item on his list was to complete a triathlon.

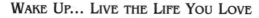

Several days later a pair of lungs compatible with Scott's blood type and genetic makeup became available. He underwent transplant surgery and received the healthy lungs. The recovery was slow and was shadowed by the constant fear of his body rejecting the new lungs. But, he consistently took his anti-rejection medications which suppressed his immune system, making organ rejection less likely. This medication also made it more difficult to fight off illness. Nevertheless, he continued to improve. While his cystic fibrosis was not cured by the transplant, he rejoiced at his chance for a longer, healthier life.

As Scott gained strength, he didn't forget his deathbed dream list. He started out by working with physical therapists and simply learning how to walk again after lying in a hospital bed for months. The walking led to swimming, biking and eventually running. After his strength was re-built, he completed his first triathlon. His number one "if I could just live" goal came true! He continued to complete triathlon after triathlon. After more triathlons than I can count, he went on to compete in an Ironman event. I don't know anyone else who has ever attempted this, much less someone with cystic fibrosis and a double lung transplant. The event involves a 2.4 mile swim and 112 mile bike ride followed by a 26.2 mile marathon run.

At this time, Scott Johnson is the only transplant recipient in the world to complete an Ironman competition; "I have cystic fibrosis, but it doesn't have me." So here is my challenge to you: write out *your* "if I could only live" list. This simple yet profound experience will help you to clarify your goals and dreams so you may begin the process of moving forward. Since yesterday is gone and tomorrow never gets here, the time is now.

Becoming a published author was at the top of my list. My career began as a healthcare provider. I wanted to improve the health of others, yet I didn't feel that I fully met my goal. I took care of about 20 patients a day, about 80 a week and more than 4,000 in a single year. It was never enough.

Eventually I began teaching future healthcare providers. If there is one thing (hopefully many more than one) I can say or do over the course of their studies that will make them a better, more caring healthcare provider, it is worth it. This is now my way of helping *more* people. In a class of 70 students, let's say they will likely each see 20 patients per day. *I have touched lives exponentially.* That's 1,400 a day, 7,000 a week and 364,000 a year. Maybe this is still not enough. Maybe this is why I'm writing this story? If I can touch your life in some small or huge way by sharing my experience with Scott, my goal has been achieved.

Scott is such an inspiration: a wonderful reminder to us all. Why should we wait until our deathbeds to have a wake-up call? It's time to stop existing and start living!

Laura Bank, Ph.D., PA-C

Waking Up from a Nightmare

John R. Jacobs

My story is about the journey of life and my discovery that sometimes hardships, struggles and losses are not always as devastating as they seem.

I grew up in a rural farming community as a member of a Mennonite family that believed in hard work, honesty and strong values. I decided very early in life that as soon as I completed grade 10, I would begin an apprenticeship to an auto mechanic and I would start taking care of myself financially so I wouldn't have to work 14 hour days as my family did. My dream and passion was to work with cars. I was very lucky to be so talented with my hands: something I noticed early on in life and clearly inherited from my father, who could literally fix anything. In 1970, I began my career as an auto mechanic.

In 1987, I decided to start my own auto repair business. It was then that I found that when we are not on the right road, the universe has a way of putting us back where we should be. If only I knew then what I know now.

To make a long story short, in 1997 I was charged with fraud for odometer tampering and vehicle misrepresentation. I went through a five year battle with the government, the courts and our justice system, who flatly told me they were trying to make an example out of me. They repeatedly told me to get out of the business. I stubbornly clung to my innocence and continued working to clear my name and get my license back. This proved futile and only increased my anger and financial losses.

Unfortunately, our society has a disturbing preoccupation with human failings. People want us to suffer, to be humiliated and to be restricted so we will never commit similar offences again. Sadly, punishment rarely accomplishes anything but pain. We punish people for their mistakes instead of seeing their mistakes as an opportunity to help them.

I suffered huge financial losses, which caused a lot of stress and embarrassment for my children, Kerri, Janelle and Craig, and my wife Beverly. During this terrible time Beverly became very ill, suffering from depression and chronic fatigue. I could not believe how my life was spiraling out of control, both personally and professionally. I became very angry and was not pleasant to be around. I turned to alcohol in a futile attempt to relieve some pain. I found myself asking the question, "Why is this happening to me?"

At some point, all of the negativity forced me to make a choice to improve my life. Either I had to try to make things better or I would continue to wallow in my misery. I started to read motivational and self-improvement books, listen to tapes and CDs and attend seminars on similar topics. Dr. Wayne Dyer became my mentor, my hero and my savior, and I was filled with a deep passion to read—something I had never had before. I could not satisfy my hunger to absorb knowledge. Dr. Dyer's work showed me "The Power of Love:" to love myself and bring love into all parts of my life. I also learned forgiveness—to forgive everyone I harbored anger toward and, most of all, to forgive myself. I had an attitude of gratitude for life and for all I have in it. I strove to become a passionate, loving, caring person. Greg Baer, author of *Real Love,* showed me that when our "Love Tank" is empty, it is impossible to show love towards others. You can only give away what is inside you, and prior to my experiences of embracing love and forgiveness, there was not very much love in my heart. To this day, I still work with the Tao meditation and breathing exercises that Dr. Dyer teaches. These exercises help me to stay calm, focused and grateful for what I have in life. They also help me to be gentle and tolerate imperfections in myself and others.

As my life was growing spiritually, profound changes began to take place. As I mentioned, my wife was ill during this time. We struggled trying to identify her illness and find the right treatment. Doctors consistently failed to help us. Bev actually learned about detoxification technology known as Ion Cleanse®: the machine pulls toxins out of the body through a footbath.

The Ion Cleanse helped my wife show great improvement in her health, returning her energy and well-being. We were all so happy we decided to share the wonderful benefits of greater health with the world. We shut down our auto repair business and founded Healthier Living 4 You, a company dedicated to bringing innovative healthcare equipment and products for personal and professional use. We started with the Ion Cleanse machine and began distributing throughout Canada. The success we had with this product led to the creation of the Ion Detox therapy machine, a product with significant improvements over the Ion Cleanse. It sold rapidly across North America, and inspired us to create a whole line of products.

I am in awe of how the Law of Attraction has affected this journey. Once I began focusing on the positive things in my life and letting go of the past, everything started showing up as needed. Not only did Bev recover from her illness, I discovered an entirely new field of work—one that is vastly more fulfilling than my previous job and which fans the flames of my passion to help people live the lives they love. Bijan, author of *Effortless Health*, says that to be in peace, we must know our only function in life is to heal ourselves and others through our expressions of love and forgiveness. Also, very recently, I completed the *Passion Test* with Chris and Janet Attwood and discovered something amazing as I wrote out *My Passions*. My first passion was to co-author a book with Wayne Dyer. I never thought I was smart enough to write a book and really didn't know it was a passion of mine until I wrote it down. My list of other passions includes: helping people heal, maintain healthy relationships, marriages, families and lives while bringing more unconditional love to every person in this world. Let's see if I can have all of these come true as well.

I have learned much during my journey, and continue to learn more everyday. Each bit of knowledge I gain and each new experience opens my eyes to how much I really don't know. Life is such a mystery—a wonderful, confusing, terrifying, joyous mystery.

I hope my story has shown you that anything is possible. You can go from the depths of despair to living the life you love. As the title of one of my favorite Wayne Dyer books says, "You will see it when you believe it."

John Jacobs

CHANGE YOUR LIFE IN 30 MINUTES

Daniel Gallapoo

When is someday going to become today? When is it going to be *your* day? Pay attention: your biggest regrets in life won't be the things you did; your biggest regrets will be the things you *didn't* do.

Trust me: those kinds of regret are kicked-in-the-gut painful. They hurt down in your soul. They can suck the life right out of you. Of all the pain I've experienced throughout my life, I can't think of a single thing more painful than regret for dreams never pursued.

Many adults have lost the ability to dream. They give up after experiencing the normal disappointments and setbacks of life, because it seems less painful to give up on their dreams and expect nothing than to hope for something and be disappointed. However, most kids haven't had the ability to dream beaten out of them yet, unless they were raised by parents with a "poverty mindset."

Whenever I talk to teenagers who have a dream—*any* kind of dream—I feel like grabbing them by the shoulders, shaking them and saying, "Please! Please! Just do it! It's a great dream! Get started now! Just put the blinders on and go for it! The worst thing that can happen is losing a little time." It's better to give the dream a shot for a few years so you can look back and know that at least you tried. It really hurts to know you had the talent, intelligence and, more importantly, the determination to achieve your dream, but never made the effort because you listened to the dream stealers. What doesn't make any sense at all is that those dream stealers will most likely be your family and friends—the very people you would think would most want your success and happiness. I don't think they do it to deliberately hurt you. I think they do it because:

1. They really believe they are giving you sound, practical advice to keep you from getting hurt or disappointed.

2. If you succeed, or even just start the *process* of pursuing a dream, it's too hard for these people to cope with because the implication is that they could do it, too. They could be pursuing their dreams and improving their lives, too, but they choose instead to spend their free time watching television or hanging out with friends. They'd rather avoid you or bring you down than be faced with your silent, daily accusation that they, too, could have a successful life.

Wouldn't it be a shame if you died without having achieved anything noteworthy? Without ever pursuing or accomplishing any of your dreams and goals?

I guess I'm unusual, but I didn't know how unusual I was until just recently. A quick poll of ten friends revealed a grand total of zero who felt anything similar. When questioned, none of them had life plans any grander than the possibility of a new plasma television or a vacation next year. No ambitions, no drive, no enthusiasm: nothing.

Imagine a life just like the billions of others before you—going to work every day in a mundane, dead-end job, sleeping, eating, mowing the lawn, washing the car until one day your number comes up and you check out of this earthly existence.

About ten billion humans have lived and died on this giant ball of mud hurtling through space. How many of those ten billion did anything noteworthy during their lives? Maybe a tenth of one percent? What about the rest? Incredibly, they were willing to waste away their irreplaceable, limited, precious life in dull, repetitive, mind-numbing boredom. And, in many cases, this was their choice—it wasn't imposed on them as it was in previous generations.

These millions of human beings left nothing behind except a new generation of the same. They're all gone now, their names forgotten. They didn't push humanity forward by even one inch. It's sad to say, but 98 percent of gravestones should simply state: *"Here lies John Doe. He was born, he wasted his nearly limitless potential doing nothing important, he died."* You think I'm kidding? Look around you. Talk to people. Do they have any burning ambitions? Any creative energy? Do they want to leave a mark? To accomplish anything with their lives? Do you know anybody who is actually taking action toward a dream, no matter how small? I doubt it. There are precious few.

There are plenty of people sitting around doing nothing but hoping their ship will someday come in to carry them to success. But I've got news for you: that ship isn't coming. You can hope, pray, cry, go through all the motions, rituals, ceremonies, recitations and chants required by your religion, or you can read a million positive thinking books and look in the mirror every morning while saying your affirmations. It doesn't matter, that ship is not coming to magically take you to success. No magical, spiritual or celestial force or being is going to float out of the sky to pull you to the realization of your dreams. The sooner you accept that, the sooner you can do what you *really* need to do to realize your dreams.

You are that ship, my dear friend. The help you are waiting for is you. Only you can do the work needed to get the ship moving forward.

Gary Halbert, my mentor in direct marketing and copywriting once told me, "Motion beats meditation." So, I have a very important question to ask you: "When are you going to get started on those dreams you've been talking about? Days have turned into weeks, months and years. And you really don't have a whole lot of time left." Can you really stomach the thought of a life filled with gut-wrenching regrets, all because you kept putting off your dream until tomorrow?

Tomorrow is today. For God's sake, set aside 30 minutes *today* to get started toward your dream—just 30 short minutes! Do something in those 30 minutes that will move you a little bit closer to that dream. Then do it again tomorrow and every day after that.

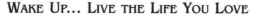

Don't squander your life waiting for "someday" to arrive. Take action now. Please don't look back at age 40, 50, 60 or older with regret for the things you didn't do. You have the power and ability to design whatever kind of life you want. I sincerely believe you can accomplish what you really determine to accomplish, but it doesn't matter if I believe it. You have to believe it and start taking action. Get started today. In fact, *right now* would be the perfect time.

Daniel Gallapoo

LIVE THE LIFE YOU LOVE—AGAIN

Ed Lacey

I believe that we all have defining moments that change the trajectory of our lives. For me, it came through experiencing the saving grace of God through His Son, Jesus Christ, and being saved from a tragic accident. We have all experienced that to some degree. We often get the wake up call first, and then the defining moment occurs. Other times, the defining moment in our lives is the wake up call.

I was 26,000 feet over Italy, flying through the clouds for 45 minutes under a canopy and living the life I loved. I was a Captain in the Special Forces with a military free fall detachment. I had previously served with the 1st Ranger Battalion, been a Company Commander of a Basic Training unit at Ft. Benning, Georgia, and years later would command the Group Support Company of the 5th Special Forces Group during Operation Desert Storm. For me, life was wonderful. My whole life revolved around military service and my wake up call came when I was informed that the Army no longer needed my service. I got caught in the downsizing of the Armed Forces in the early '90s. Tony Robbins would say that I had let that define who I was, but that's for another chapter. So there I was, at the end of a very successful military career with no Plan B.

An interesting thing about life and a person's journey of self-discovery and development is that an answer always seems to appear at the right moment. Most of us have heard the old saying, "When the student is ready, the teacher will appear." In my case, that is exactly what happened.

One of the guys I served with told me I should hear something a friend of his had to say. He invited me over for pizza and the three of us sat down and his friend began to explain a wonderful business opportunity. Many of you have probably had a similar experience, but you discovered it was network marketing and immediately turned it down. Fortunately for me, I kept listening and this is what I discovered: network marketing is one of the last level playing fields in business. It doesn't matter what your background is, how much experience you have, your education, age, gender, race or creed. Compared to traditional businesses, the start-up investment is small, and the potential for returns is unlimited. It is about helping others and being part of a team that is something bigger than yourself.

If you are not receiving residual income for doing something only once and continuing to get paid for it over and over again; if you have not learned the secret of leveraging your time and money; and/or if you do not have a plan B, I would strongly encourage you to take a serious look at the often misunderstood industry of network marketing. This book is about living the life you love, and no other industry out there is more about self-development, team development, and lifestyle than network marketing.

It has been said that network marketing is a self-development program with a compensation package attached. The reason why people like Donald Trump or Robert Kiyosaki would encourage it is because it works as a business model and it is a great business education program to develop the individual entrepreneur. It has been said that not all business men/women are entrepreneurs, but all entrepreneurs are business men/women. The old objections of not being a sales person are easily dealt with in the industry, but don't get me wrong: if you love sales or are extremely good at selling, then you will probably love network marketing. The industry is about the individual more than anything else. As it is said in the industry, "Network marketing is right for everyone, but not everyone is right for network marketing."

There are countless stories of how, after becoming involved with this industry, a person's life was totally changed. Many times you'll find people involved in network marketing who are not there for the monetary gain, but for the great friends they have made and the people they have met. The personal growth it offers can be compared to an MBA in life. Stories of transformation—such as the shy housewife who is petrified of standing in front of a group of five people who becomes a self-confident person giving a presentation to 10,000 people at the annual convention—are not uncommon. This is an industry of lifestyle. I don't know of any other businesses where you can take off on a vacation for a month and return to an income that has doubled or tripled. But don't be fooled: this is netWORK marketing. Unfortunately, people forget that—just like any other business, you have to work hard to see results. That scenario doesn't happen to the person just starting out, but it can and *does* happen to a strong, mature organization that has been developed through blood, sweet and tears. So, the next time you hear about network marketing, don't turn it down too soon. Keep listening and look for a connection, then go for it.

Life is too short not to be doing what you love. Take this book and the stories within it to inspire you to wake up, make any changes that need to be made in your life, and start living the life you love. Life is to be lived to the fullest—it isn't a dress rehearsal. I love the lyrics to Kenny Chesney's song "Don't Blink:" "'Cause when your hourglass runs out of sand, you can't flip it over and start again, take every breath God gives you for what it's worth."

It has been my privilege to share my experience with you. May you live the life you love and live it to its fullest.

Ed Lacey

EMBRACE SILENCE

Dr. Wayne Dyer

You live in a noisy world, constantly bombarded with loud music, sirens, construction equipment, jet airplanes, rumbling trucks, leaf blowers, lawn mowers and tree cutters. These manmade, unnatural sounds invade your senses and keep silence at bay.

In fact, you've been raised in a culture that not only eschews silence, but is terrified of it. The car radio must always be on, and any pause in conversation is a moment of embarrassment that most people quickly fill with chatter. For many, being alone in silence is pure torture.

The famous scientist Blaise Pascal observed, "All man's miseries derive from not being able to sit quietly in a room alone."

With practice, you can become aware that there's a momentary silence in the space between your thoughts. In this silent space, you'll find the peace that you crave in your daily life. You'll never know that peace if you don't have any spaces between your thoughts.

The average person is said to have 60,000 separate thoughts a day. With so many thoughts, there are almost no gaps. If you could reduce that number by half, you would open up an entire world of possibilities for yourself. For it is when you merge into the silence, and become one with it, that you reconnect to your source and know the peacefulness that some call "God." It is stated beautifully in Psalms of the Old Testament: "Be still and know that I am God." The key words are "still" and "know."

"Still" actually means "silence." Mother Teresa described silence and its relationship to God by saying, "God is the friend of silence. See how nature (trees, grass) grows in silence. We need silence to be able to touch souls." This includes your soul.

It's really the space between the notes that make the music you enjoy so much. Without the spaces, all you would have is one continuous, noisy note. Everything that's created comes out of silence. Your thoughts emerge from the nothingness of silence. Your words come out of this void. Your very essence emerged from emptiness.

All creativity requires some stillness. Your sense of inner peace depends on spending some of your life energy in silence to recharge your batteries, removing tension and anxiety, thus reacquainting you with the joy of knowing God and feeling closer to all of humanity. Silence reduces fatigue and allows you to experience your own creative juices.

The second word in the Old Testament observation, "know," refers to making your personal and conscious contact with God. To know God is to banish doubt and become independent of others' definitions and descriptions of God. Instead, you have your own personal knowing. And, as Melville reminded us so poignantly, "God's one and only voice is silence."

Dr. Wayne Dyer

WAKING UP TO "YES"

Raul G. Rodriguez, M.D.

There are times in life when nothing seems to go right. In times like these, despair and frustration darken every day. Against all odds, I found myself in such a situation following a financial disaster that threatened the very core of my being. All of my dreams were shattered and everything I valued was gone. My professional and family life was affected in ways I never anticipated. The only bright light was the support of my wife and the understanding from my children.

Even though I had my professional degree, my hope for recovery was limited. The tasks of daily living were difficult to finish, followed by long, sleepless nights. Dealing with the situation was challenging. My mind was working overtime with very little success. Because of my upbringing, it was difficult to share my feelings, and seeking help was just out of the question. From the depths of my despair, I searched for answers to my predicament and for direction in my life.

The answers came to me in 1994. I was reading chapter 16 of the *Big Book of Alcoholics Anonymous*. In an instant that felt like an eternity, my mind went very quiet. There were no thoughts. Nothing appeared. I had never experienced such silence in my life. While experiencing this silence, I received a loving and compassionate message: "Say yes to everything. Acceptance is the answer to all of your problems." Even though the words were the ones written in the book, their meaning became absolutely clear to me. It was an epiphany that transformed my life. Words cannot convey the experience.

I experienced immense love, my fears disappeared, and in the core of my being, I knew those words were true. I did not know what this experience was all about, and all I could do was let go of the desire to explain it. It transformed my life and that was all that mattered. It was not an easy task for my scientifically trained mind to cease trying to explain this phenomenon. My only option was to say "yes" to what was occurring. The meaning to me was this: Things are as they are, and they are not as they are not. I realized that disagreeing with reality was only a losing proposition.

This truth changed my life in unexpected ways. The consistent application of this new truth helped me move forward from despair to hope, from financial disaster to abundance, from mediocrity to excellence, from chaos to peace, and from a busy mind to a quiet mind. From the moment of my new self-discovery, I adopted this as my new professional philosophy: treat mental illness, but promote mental health. As a fresh reflection of my newly acquired mental stillness, I changed the name of my practice to Stillpoint Medical Group.

I would like to say that after this experience my life changed instantly, but that was not the case. It took time. Learning to say "yes" to everything happening in my life challenged my experiences, tested my belief system and aroused negativity I did not know existed in me. It helped me confront feelings and emotions buried deep in my soul. Today, I am a transformed man. During the transformation period, many people came into my life. Some supported my efforts and encouraged my progress, while others confronted my shortcomings and helped me to open up to new perspectives. Others offered generous and invaluable advice. To all, I am grateful.

Through the years, I have found that saying "yes" to what *is* gets me back to the same quietness of mind, where there are no needs and no desires. On the other hand, saying no gets me to a state of distress, dissatisfaction and unrest. The process is so simple, and yet, so profound.

Those who give themselves permission to say yes to what is, reap wonderful benefits, improve their relationships, enhance their finances, increase their productivity and align themselves to whatever they want. A problem no longer remains a problem when it is totally and unconditionally accepted. Try it: you will like it.

How can I make such claims? I have coached many people with all manner of serious emotional and physical problems. By using this simple understanding, I have seen positive results. Either the problem disappears, the suffering associated with the problem dissipates, or the quality of the person's life is such that the problem does not seem important any longer.

Try it. What I suggest at this moment is to repeat the word "yes" several times. Do you notice any kind of reaction? The reaction usually comes in the form of a thought, an image, or a sensation in your body. Whatever the reaction, say "yes" to it. Yes means permission to be, agreement or consent. Do not judge your reaction. You do not need to do anything. Simply say "yes" to what is happening.

Now, repeat the word "no" several times. Is there any reaction? How similar or dissimilar is your reaction from when you said "yes"? Whatever the reaction is, could you allow it to be? Again, do not judge your reaction. Simply allow it to be.

Saying "yes" is expansive, encompassing, compassionate, tolerant, accepting and non-judgmental. It brings love, peace and freedom. Saying "no", on the other hand, is constrictive, judgmental, arrogant and rejecting. It brings pain and suffering, and keeps love, peace and freedom away.

Become aware of which answer feels better and make a conscious choice to use only that one. With practice, your skill will improve and a general sense of well-being will make its presence felt. Do it: you will like it.

Practice saying "yes" to any person in your life. Think about someone. Could you say "yes" to this person? Could you say yes to the thoughts you have about this person? Good, bad or indifferent? Could you say "yes" to the feelings you have about this person? Could you say "yes" to any reaction you may have toward this person? Practice this exercise with everyone with whom you are in frequent contact. It may take some time, but the resulting experience can change your life. Your relationships and your love life will greatly improve.

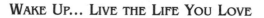

Could you say YES to your current state of health?
Could you say YES to your current financial situation?
Could you say YES to your current occupation?
Could you say YES to the current state of world affairs?
Could you say YES to the current climate condition?
Could you say YES to world peace?
Could you say YES to being married?
Could you say YES to being single?
Could you say YES to the now feelings about the thoughts crossing your mind?
Could you say YES to…? (Add anything and everything you can think of that is happening in your world).

The possibilities are limitless. Practice frequently. The rewards may be unimaginable to you until you experience the results firsthand. Don't believe a word I say: prove it to yourself. Prove that you can have peace, abundance, happiness and freedom.

The life of abundance, peace of mind and joy I live today exemplifies the application of this principle. My prayer is for you to reap the same results.

Raul G. Rodriguez, M.D.

A LESSON FROM J.R. EWING

Dominique (Nicky) Viard

For as long as I can remember, I have had a very contentious relationship with my father. He tended to be envious, controlling and dictatorial. He was resentful of my very existence and felt threatened by my questioning mind and refusal to submit to his demands for unearned admiration. I had an extraordinary sense of morality from a young age and I was always fighting him tooth and nail on right and wrong. I never understood cruel and emotionally abusive people. I believed they had no mission other than to feed, like vampires, off the vibrancy of others—until one day. This experience may seem trivial, but for me it became one of the greatest "ah-ha!" moments of my life.

In 1991, I sat down to watch the series finale of the TV show *Dallas*. In this episode, the infamous J.R. Ewing was actually having a moment of conscience, realizing that he had ruined many lives and, at best, had caused a great deal of heartache. At this time, his guardian angel, Adam, materializes and takes J.R. on a *Christmas Carol* journey. Adam shows J.R. what everyone's life would have been like had he never existed. As one could imagine, many lives were better as a result of his non-existence, but some fared worse. Most notably was that of his younger brother, Bobby.

Instead of the happily-married, powerful and successful businessman the audience knew him to be, in this alternate reality, Bobby is a penniless, irresponsible and cowardly playboy who is up to his eyeballs in debts with bullying loan sharks. J.R. did, in fact, love his brother, so he was quite shocked—almost to the point of tears—as he demanded to know what had happened to the strong, courageous, upstanding Bobby that he knew and respected.

The answer to J.R.'s inquiry was one I will never forget. Adam replied that it was because of J.R. himself that Bobby became the powerful, moral fighter that J.R. knew him to be. It was constantly fighting J.R. that gave

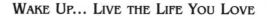

Bobby direction, giving him the strength and rectitude that J.R. knew him to have.

At that moment, I cried and cried as everything became clear. Everyone exists for a purpose, including those who are evil. We fight, and it makes us strong and noble. I quickly realized I had been made better by it. Perpetually fighting evil helped me develop moral "biceps," which I would not have without this heavy burden that I lifted on a daily basis. In his own way, my father made me stronger, wiser and more fit for life, just as J.R. had for Bobby. My father made me deeply passionate in ways no one else could, which is how I learned one of the most enduring lessons of my life. And you know what? My Dad was made better for it, too.

Dominique (Nicky) Viard

How I Found My Destiny and Passion

Ashok P. Nair

As a young boy growing up in a village in India, I never dreamed that one day I would be writing from the most prosperous North American continent. What was the driving force behind my journey? I didn't know then, but I understand now.

It was not easy to reach this point while enjoying my career as a teacher, making positive changes in the lives of others. People said throughout my life I was a rolling stone, but this rolling stone has a story.

It Was All About Choices

No matter what choices you make in life, you must face their consequences. I was not ready to face the consequences, and the results were painful. On Jan. 15, 1998, I got an interview in Canada. I was overjoyed someone had finally called me for an interview after I sent out more than 500 résumés. Interviews are now fun for me, but 10 years ago, I would panic just hearing the word. Thanks to God, after the years of self-help workshops, meditation, Yoga, counseling and Reiki, I changed my personality and outlook.

The interview went very well, but my joy was short-lived once I learned about my responsibilities. I was to do door-to-door fund-raising for a community service organization for a wage of $7.00 per hour. Having obtained my master's degree in organic chemistry from one of the most prestigious universities in India, in addition to a management degree, coupled with several years experience as a professor, marketing consultant, educational consultant, along with work experience in multinational companies, this job offer was a bit disappointing.

It had been eight months since I landed in Canada, and since I had been unsuccessful finding any other employment, I took the job. On the first day I was dropped off on a street in Calgary at about 6:00 p.m. I was to knock on doors and ask for donations. It was so cold that I couldn't even speak properly. I started knocking, and it dawned on me that this was going to be a tough job. My pen would freeze, and when I took off my gloves, my fingers felt so cold, pain would shoot to my bones.

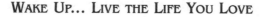

When I reached the tenth house, an elderly lady opened the door. I felt so cold that my jaws were jammed and I could not talk. The lady asked me, "My dear, you seem to be from another country. Do you know what the temperature is outside?" I said, "No, ma'am." "Well, my child," she said, "you should be resting at home, as it is -37 degrees Celsius outside." I was speechless as my years in chemistry research came to my mind. Sub-zero temperature! I was finished.

For two days, my fingers bled from frostbite and I couldn't get out of my bed. "Why is this happening to me?" I kept on asking God, "What did I do?" During those two days in bed, I contemplated my situation. Finally, I realized something.

When I was small, I enjoyed watching movies with snow and I often wished to be in such a place. It looks like my wish was fulfilled even if it wasn't exactly what I wanted. Maybe I should have been clearer.

I was fortunate to get acquainted with a friend who invited me to stay with his family. His children were in 10th and 11th grade, and I was a great help to them. His family enjoyed my presence, and I became a part of them. However, when I crawled into my bed, I was back to my old self. There were nights when I cried myself to sleep. I was all alone and depressed.

It was during this time that my visions became clearer and I began contemplating my life's purpose. Each day I spent hours in introspection and meditation. Once, I came across a famous psychic who told me I was gifted in many ways, but that I was not accepting God's gift. He said I should be a teacher, motivating people and spreading happiness, because I have a lot to contribute to society. He was the first one who said I must make use of my Reiki Mastery, years of international work experience, hypnotherapy certification and rich spiritual experience. He also said I would get a break when we got snow in Calgary. He said it would just be a job to make ends meet, and I had a great journey ahead, but I did not have the confidence to believe him then.

Initially there were no signs of a job. Then I got a call for an interview for the following day. Unfortunately, I didn't have any money left to get to the interview, so I prayed and waited. The next morning, I received $24 in the mail from the door-to-door marketing company for the one night job I did. I was thankful from the deepest part of my heart.

By the end of October, it had snowed and the psychic's prediction came true. I got a real job in Canada, this time for a manpower agency hiring 45 workers for a new Canadian tire store. I was hired and was asked to get steel-toed boots and a hard hat, neither of which I had ever heard of. Somehow, I purchased them and my new career as a laborer began. It was a humbling experience, because in our culture, this kind of job was for uneducated people.

In Tears, My Wake-Up Moment Arrives

That night, the universe, along with my confidence, brought up a memory about an event that occurred when I was about 4 or 5 years old. My destiny was decided then, but I had totally forgotten about it. My father's friend, a renowned priest and Vedic pundit, came to our house and showed me the Divine Power. There, in a vessel of water, was the live form of the Monkey God Hanuman who showed me I was to be a teacher by writing it on a blackboard. Then, the image disappeared.

I struggled for 30 years to remember that incident, and when I came out of my meditation, I realized I was crying. How could I have forgotten my destiny to be a teacher? I understood there were opportunities behind every problem I faced. Only when I was ready to look beyond them and accept the consequences of my choices did the message dawn on me.

This was the birth of a new person who was willing to forget the past, learn from mistakes and live in the present. A teacher is born to learn continuously from both positive and negative experiences. The moment I accepted this truth, life changed for me and every day is new. I thank God for showering me with His love and kindness. Let your opportunities and problems be your teachers so you can get in touch with your true self and live out your dreams.

Ashok P. Nair

SYNCHRONIZED INTENTION

Len Z. Nichols

Are you willing to receive a wake up call that could change your life, or will you allow another opportunity to pass you by?

Wake up moments always arrive unexpectedly, charged with a personal meaningfulness. In order to recognize and appreciate these moments of synchronicity, however, you must learn to respect your intuition. Awakening to intuition is a gradual process, yet each new insight comes suddenly.

I wrote and published the book *Saving The Planet From Ourselves: Our Awakening is Just Around the Bend* to share a deepening realization: simply focusing on self, family, culture and country is no longer sufficient. The present global context demands a larger, more meaningful commitment—a commitment to valuing the whole of humanity and the planet itself.

However, I chose to withhold the underlying intuition and synchronized intention that informed my writing. At the time, I thought that discussing personal epiphanies would only give the reader unnecessary reason to question my credibility. Fear prevented me from fully spreading my wings. Like a caterpillar—ready, but refusing to leave the comfort of the cocoon—I chose to hide my expanding consciousness.

Suddenly another "wake up moment" changed everything. My wife, Louise, and I were in Vancouver's International Airport. We had just visited our son, Jason, and had given him a suitcase full of my books to distribute. A few months earlier, I had sent books to humanitarians and ecologically concerned celebrities and writers in hopes of collaborating with a major publisher to distribute the book globally. I had received a response from everyone but one—*Seat of the Soul* author, Gary Zukav. I was preoccupied with why he had not gotten back to me.

Louise's voice was firm with resolve, "Let it go, Len, you're obsessing! You felt drawn to bring Jason books. And you did. You've done your part—let it go and see what happens!"

Louise left me to watch our luggage while she went to the restroom. I made my way to a nearby vendor to get a cup of coffee. A man stopped me, "Excuse me, do you know what time it is?"

"No, I don't have a wristwatch," I said as I scanned the walls for a clock. "There," I pointed to a clock and told him the time.

The man thanked me and I watched him take a seat at a nearby boarding gate. I smiled at the timing of his question. At that very moment, I was thinking about airport security and concluded: It's time we all woke up!

But the matter continued to occupy my mind: Of all the people in the airport, why did he ask me? I wasn't wearing a wristwatch. I felt a strange urgency to speak with this man. Although I had only seen dated pictures of him, his resemblance to Gary Zukav was remarkable.

"Stop it! Get a grip on yourself!" I told myself. "What do you think: that you just conjured him up?"

"But what if he is Gary Zukav? You'll kick yourself later if you don't have the courage to check it out."

Louise returned and I immediately stood up. "Where are you going?" She asked.

"I'm going to talk with a guy." I certainly wasn't going to tell Louise what I was up to. She'd think I'd flipped my lid.

Two years earlier, I had a dream that Gary and I were promoting world peace on Oprah's show. The dream inspired me to send him a draft of my manuscript. It was promptly returned with a note from an assistant: "Gary does not accept any unsolicited manuscripts." So, I waited to send him a published copy.

After an awkward moment, I said, "I'm the guy you asked about the time. Are you Gary Zukav?"

"Yes," he said with a smile.

"I'm in awe!" I blurted out. "Not with you…or with me, but with the process, the synchronicity. I've been trying to collaborate with you for a couple of years now. But you have an administrative assistant to prevent people like me from reaching you." I realized that my inappropriate giddiness could blow this opportunity. So, I excused myself to get the only copy of the book I had with me. This copy was missing a page—the sole reason I had not left it with Jason.

Louise dug it out of her carry-on-bag, "What are you doing?" "I'm talking with Gary Zukav," I replied in a heightened state of awareness. "Oh, sure," Louise mocked. I could only smile and shake my head, "I'll be right back."

I handed Gary the book, as I articulated its holistic goal—a planet free of nuclear weapons. Gary said he would forward my book to his literary agent. He smiled, "If it goes…it goes." I introduced Gary to Louise. If Louise did not meet Gary, how could she believe that this had actually happened?

Three months later, I received a detailed letter from Gary's agent: "These pages contain a wonderful message, but…I think an editor would feel that the project didn't bring enough that was new or add a fresh enough perspective to the other books that are already out there. In spite of these pages' strengths, I'd better pass."

Of course he had to pass. After all, I passed up the opportunity to articulate the fresh moments of synchronicity that inspired my writing, the story behind the story. This important feedback encouraged me to begin writing about the very personal journey of how my heart and awareness awoke in stages. The working title of this book (in progress) is *Adventures in Awakening: Expanding Awareness.*

Shortly afterward, I joyfully jumped at the opportunity to share how I awoke to my life's purpose in *Wake Up...Live The Life You Love: A Search for Purpose.* And now, I am grateful to express my heightened reverence for intuition and synchronicity in this collection of *Wake Up Moments!*

Most people are oblivious to the natural synchronistic flow of energy. Many resist it. You can easily block your ability to access wake up moments by:

1) Expecting a specific type of resolution, based on your own limited, self-centered understanding.
2) Insisting that a solution take place on your terms and within your time frame.

For many years, I successfully blocked myself in these ways. Today, however, my daily practice involves feeling grateful for the ability to celebrate our interdependence and connectedness and to experience a sense of "oneness." I continually seek a deeper level of compassion for myself, for others, and for all of humanity as we struggle to expand awareness along our developmental journey. The more I appreciate living from moment to moment in compassion, love and forgiveness, the more my awareness unfolds.

Life is an unfathomable mystery. But what an exciting adventure—especially if you actively listen to your intuition and joyfully act on moments of synchronicity. To do this, you must give yourself permission to awaken to a greater reality. Then, by allowing yourself to expect the unexpected, you can awaken in a way that is personally meaningful to you!

Len Z. Nichols

LISTENING FOR GOD (FROM THE WAKE UP LIVE MOVIE)

Zachary Levi

My "Wake Up Moment" was when I realized how much God loved me and that there were things in my life that I wanted to do and things I felt like God had made me do. He wasn't keeping things from me because He was mad at me; He was keeping them from me because He knew that I wasn't ready for them. When I realized that, and when I realized that He wanted to bless me with those things, and I was getting my life together, then it all started falling into place. And so, my "Wake Up Moment" was knowing God's love.

So I would just tell young professionals of any kind to make sure you know why you want it. Is it because you really love the art of it, is it because you're really into the fame and the fortune? Know your motives as best you can, and know your passions as best you can. If you are really passionate about it, you will go forward and succeed. You know, it's almost not even a choice.

So, it's not as if you're asking, "Should I be an actor?" It's "I have to be an actor, or a musician," or whatever the case may be.

But you also have to know that this may not be what you are ultimately supposed to do. Maybe it's just something you're supposed to pursue for a time that will bring you somewhere else. It should never be about who you are. It doesn't define you. You could go off to be the next Wolfgang Puck, but you never would have found that if you hadn't come to Hollywood and tried to be an actor. So always be open to wherever God is taking you.

Zachary Levi

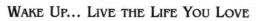

SPIRITUAL SPEED BUMPS

Jon Stetson

"Hello. My name is Jon Stetson and I like to feel good."

It's true. Each year I present my signature program, The Stetson Experience™, at hundreds of events, from the White House to corporate and social gatherings. At these events I demonstrate how the amazing powers within the human psyche can inspire and teach others to achieve more, be more effective and—simply put—to *feel good.* With over 30 years of performing experience in more than 23 countries, I've been blessed through hard work and plenty of luck to achieve success in a business where competition abounds and the rewards are great. However, I certainly didn't start at the top. My first paying "gig" was as a nine-year-old Cub Scout. Later, my education continued as I learned about life and human nature as a bartender, cruise director, talent agent, event planner, magician, busker, actor, comedian, comedy writer, producer, director, consultant and member of the National Speakers Association, as well as Meeting Planners International.

For a long time, despite my success, I never really felt good. I was suffering from depression; I knew I was on the wrong road when I looked forward to the end of the show rather then the performance itself—something I had always lived for.

Doing the unique work that I do—working with people's innermost thoughts, hopes and dreams to inspire them—is what finally gave me a glimpse into the inner world we all share as human beings. I was feeling those internal obstacles that keep us all unhappy, but I thought they were unique to me, until I started down this fascinating road where others opened up and let me see that we are all in this existence together; that we all share more than any of us ever thought possible.

Now I feel good. First of all, I'm aware that anyone reading an "inspirational" book such as this will be bombarded by more metaphors than a four-year-old has questions. Often the reader's eyes will glaze over while wondering if this story is just the same as another he or she just read. However, there is one metaphor I'm sure you'll remember. It's an "Ah ha" moment that has turned out to be one of the most valuable forces in my life. It's what I refer to fondly as a "spiritual speed bump."

I'll bet you're asking yourself right now, "Why did he write 'fondly'? Other than an automobile mechanic, who would have positive feelings about a speed bump?" I do, and here's why.

I was booked to perform at a high-pressure corporate seminar on the west coast—something that used to excite me, but by that time it struck me as just one more empty annoyance in my life. Getting into my car to drive to the airport for a six-hour flight wasn't exactly at the top of the list of things I wanted to do at that very moment. I felt I had no good options. Life seemed to be putting one spiritual speed bump after another in my path. Besides feeling used and unappreciated, I just couldn't stop thinking that I was like a cynic at a positive thinking seminar, spouting one thing while living another—feeling guilty about feeling guilty. The mental image that had formed in my mind was that I was being guided by fate and circumstance to be a trained monkey whose job was to shimmy up a tree and bring down the shiniest coconut for my master. This was not a good place to be, but I was suddenly jarred out of my self-absorbed reality by an actual speed bump that I hadn't noticed while cruising along with my internalized state of mind. My vehicle shook and rattled like a roller coaster. I instinctively stopped the car to make sure everything was alright. I started to curse at the obstacle that had so rudely interrupted my thought process while adding insult to my injury.

Then I saw it. An unexpected movement off to my right grabbed my attention. A basketball came bouncing across the street a few yards ahead where I had stopped. It didn't register at first, but then there was a blur of color and the sound of two teenage boys jostling with each other, oblivious to the world as they chased after the ball. I shuddered when I com-

prehended the tragedy that had been narrowly averted. For me, it was a life-changing experience. I've never looked at a speed bump of any type as anything other than a spiritual gift from that moment on. I had a major attitude adjustment that literally altered the way I look at life itself!

If you ask people about speed bumps, you'll hear comments such as, "They get in your way," "slow you down," "cause damage" and most of all, "They can't be ignored!" They are just another frustrating part of modern life designed to make our lives more difficult. But there's a positive side as well: All the road signs, complicated electronics and flashing lights in the world won't do a thing for those who should—but don't—pay attention to them. Yet, speed bumps save lives and achieve their purpose so simply and effectively that one could almost call it *elegant*.

Now, just as you don't want a speed bump on every street, you don't want to set up spiritual speed bumps in all areas of your "psychic" life, either. Your intuition should be left as unhindered as possible so it is free to deal with those thousands of moment-to-moment decisions we all make in our lives every day even if we aren't consciously aware of them.

In areas where caution, careful consideration or intense focusing of the intuition is needed, spiritual speed bumps can be your best friends for protecting yourself and others from both physical and spiritual harm.

I've grown to realize that the spiritual speed bumps are often our truest friends and guardian angels. They come into our lives at moments when we need to slow down and use caution. Often, it is our intuition that is calling out to us to reconsider the road we are taking and warning us that danger may lurk in unexpected circumstances.

Knowing that we have a friend with us at all times, knowing our intuition takes in everything and gives us what we need as long as we're open to the possibility and choose to listen—that can help all of us to *feel good!*

Jon Stetson

LIVE LIFE OUT LOUD!

Cutressa M. Williams

Wake up and live! Wow! How awesome that I am able to participate in a project that describes me literally! I have, as Tony Robbins says, "awakened the giant within," and I intend to live my life to its absolute fullest: with passion and reckless abandonment, I completely give myself over to God's perfect will for me and intend to take big bites out of life every moment of every single day.

My Lord, Jesus Christ, paid a very precious price to give me life, according to the New Testament verse John 10:10b. His desire for me is abundant life until it overflows my cup. To show my appreciation for His sacrifice, I am obligated to make my one life to live everything it can be and more.

Prior to my awakening, I merely existed. I would not have admitted that at the time, but it was true. I had a job, but I desired to go into business for myself. However, I allowed the fear of the unknown to stop me from taking decisive action. I tried several times to be a business owner, but I was merely playing the role and was not being my true self. I wanted to have reached millionaire status by my 30th birthday, but I was over three and a half years behind in my plan. My precious baby girl, Aspen, was in the state's horrible foster care system and, of course, I wanted her home with me. Going through that experience changed me in ways I could not have anticipated. Then my mother, for whom I had been caring, passed away the Sunday before Thanksgiving of 2007. My grandmother, who raised me and was my best friend, passed away April 3, 2006, one month before Aspen was—literally—stolen from me. Thousands of dollars and hours were spent working to bring her home.

I thank my mother for propelling me into this wonderful life that I am continuing to create daily. She was a wonderful lady, so kind and generous of heart, but she had much regret in her life. She regretted decisions from her past, which put a damper on her present and shortened her future. During the last months of her life, she was in and out of the hospital for weeks on end, yet the doctors were still unable to tell us the source of the problems. They simply threw more medications at her, which only caused more problems. It was a relief for her and me when she passed on from this life of pain and disappointment. I thank God that she planned accordingly for me and Aspen and left us an inheritance to assist us toward building our abundant life.

Every time I write a check, I think of her and thank God for her. She was a blessing to me in life and now afterward. I feel good because I know she is with Jesus and is urging me on to live out loud on purpose!

The past is now the past and I have control over my present condition and my future. I am awake and living the life I love. I work for myself as a business consultant. Abundant Success Institute & Consulting, LLC is the consulting and speaking practice I have long desired. It has pushed me headlong into my desired multi-millionaire status goal in a few short years. I am also a profitable real estate investor, online marketer, author and writer and have my own radio show. I am a law student at California School of Law, a unique and incredible online law school. I will graduate and take the California Bar Exam in autumn 2011. Acquiring my law degree is the first step toward my ultimate goal of being the first black female governor of Alabama.

Because you picked up this book of collected stories about living the life you love, you are also a person of action and conviction. You desire greatness and expect things to work for you, according to your goals and dreams. I encourage you to embrace your life and make it the absolute best it can possibly be. Change is good! If the way you are doing things now is not working, then do something different. Courage is moving in the right direction. Fear is staying put just because that is the way things have always been done. If you remember only one point from my story, let it be this: forget what others think. Do not spend your life trying to please everyone else, and in the process, not living at all.

Thank you for taking precious time out of your life to read my story. I hope it has inspired you to dream bigger and to start, if you have not already, to live your life out loud!

Say, *"Today is the first day of the best days of my life. I am courageous and will live my one life to its absolute fullest today! Now is the best time for me to act, therefore I take decisive action in the direction of my ultimate dreams today!"*

Cutressa M. Williams

LISTEN TO THE GREAT SPIRIT

Dr. Gerald W. Lizer

As I sit here in my home office, I look back and wonder how this all came about. Just where have I been and where I am going with this life of mine? My firm has been in practice for more than 30 years, and I have seen great changes occur in my life that affected those I work with every day. One of the biggest of these events occurred about 12 years ago when I was introduced to a new technology that altered the way I see patients and how I look at those I serve on a daily basis.

As I brought the technology into my office, the first person it affected was my wife. For five years, she could not raise her arm, but this new device changed that. You see, for years I felt that a higher power was very interested in what I was doing and would give me direction if I would listen. Well, I felt this new technology was given to me to help more people regain their health. It was as if He was saying, "Here is something I want you to work with that will impact the human family." It did just that.

The final event that changed my life happened like this: a patient came from California to see his family. He had Crohn's disease, and he was brought into my office by his parents. We treated him over the relatively short duration of seven visits. He went home and the doctor who had previously planned to perform his surgery cancelled because the patient no longer needed it. To say he was placed in my office by a higher power is an understatement.

We all have that same ability to heal if we will just open up and listen to our inner voice. It is inside all of us to help guide our lives and touch those we come in contact with every day. We have much to be thankful for if we will simply open our hearts and allow that higher power to show us the path we should follow. As I look back on my life, I can see it has been directed. God can make so much more of us if we just allow him to be a part of it. The older I get, the more I need directions to stay on the right path.

Stop and listen. What do you hear? That small voice is talking to you. It takes practice, but with work, anyone can train himself to hear it. The rewards for this are great, and they last for a very long time—forever, in fact. Now, I didn't say it would be easy, but it will be worth it.

We are human and we all fall, but there is always someone there to pick us up. Remember that when you pick up someone, you are being of great service. You never know where it will take you. Someday we will look back and see how many people were there for us.

Now it is your turn to grow beyond the border you have placed around yourself—become a new you. Those borders are really not there. We only think they are because of what our experience has taught us.

Good luck with your new life. Remember, the problems you deal with are meant to help you grow and not to beat you up.

Dr. Gerald W. Lizer

WEALTH FOR ETERNITY

Terri Bowersock

As a young girl in school, even though I was voted the kid least likely to succeed because I am dyslexic, I was determined not to let my disability affect what I could do. As a child, I always retreated to my bedroom to draw houses, restaurants and offices—even my own store. I told my mom that when I grew up, I wanted to own my own store.

In 1979, at the age of 19, I made my dream a reality and started Terri's Consign and Design Furnishings. I got the idea while I was visiting my father in Kansas and met some ladies who had a small consignment accessory store. I called my mother in Phoenix and said, "We're going to be rich. We're going to open a consignment furniture store!" She said, "We're going to be Sanford and Son?" I said, "No, we're going to sell gently used high-end furniture." So I got busy with my crayons and colored pencils and designed my business plan.

I borrowed $2,000 from my grandmother, my mother's living room set and opened our first store. Then, I rolled out 16 more stores nationwide with sales of $36 million. The stores are 20,000 square feet each and are filled with brand names like Thomasville, Ethan Allen and Hendredon, just to name a few. Terri's became famous for its gently used furniture, art decor, electronics, collectables and much more. When people first walked into the store, they didn't even realize the inventory was gently used. That's because I promised my mom we would have a designer look and not a Sanford and Son look. With all this success, Mom and I were living the American dream.

In 2005, my world went spiraling out of control. My mother, who was not only my business partner but also my best friend, disappeared and was believed to have been kidnapped by her boyfriend and left somewhere in the desert between Phoenix and Tucson. Two days after she went missing, I believe she sent me a message in a dream to help me locate her. In my dream, I saw myself lying in a desert river bed and saw a sand dune with a single armed saguaro cactus standing straight up above me. I could see another sand dune just on the other side of me and then I heard the coyotes howling. I heard them panting and heard their claws clicking over the rocks as they got closer and closer. When they took a nip at my fingers, I jumped up in bed terrified and vowed to find her. I got in touch with the newspapers and TV stations to ask the public to help me search. Every week, about 50 to 150 people would show up to help. Then, with mid-summer, the temperature rose to a searing 120 degrees. That's when it was only me and five other loyal employees who continued the search. Finally, after 390 days, with odds of one in a million we found her!

She was found in a dried out river bed with a single arm saguaro cactus standing above her and sand dunes on both sides. Yes, it was exactly what I saw in my dreams. Following her disappearance, my mother's boyfriend, who was the last person known to be seen with her and allegedly responsible her disappearance, committed suicide. Later, the police discovered he had a shady background that included a prison sentence and a reputation of scamming wealthy, smart and beautiful women out of their fortunes. I dubbed him "the charming predator," for stalking my mother, taking her money and her life.

If that wasn't tragic enough, I returned to my business at Terri's just to find out more bad news. The accountant told me an executive had stolen all the books and we were missing two million dollars. To make matters worse, we only had two more weeks to keep the business open. That night I went home and felt so numb, I went outside and leaned up against the house and slid down to the ground. I sat there for hours, staring off to space saying to myself, "God, just take me outta here." Finally at 4 a.m. I felt a sense of being gone. I didn't really know for how long. Then all of sudden, I came back and realized I had a message in my mind:

1. You are here to evolve and learn from your life lessons. There are no accidents!

2. What's losing two million dollars to eternity? Nothing!

3. As you build your wealth for life, make sure to build your wealth for eternity by loving yourself and others, without judging. To forgive is divine.

4. Live your life on purpose!

When I was younger, my brother and I were living with my mother who had been divorced. We had limited resources so we understood the concept of reduce, recycle and reuse. I was always cutting napkins in half, turning off the lights and saving water. As I got older I resold my items at garage sales. Reusing is my life purpose! Now I am living it. It was time to build the biggest chain across the country and to keep our planet green everywhere. I am building a chain of franchise consignment malls to provide the public a professional, easy way to resell everything from fashion to furnishings to promote the concept of buying gently used. When you buy a used table, you save four to eight trees! So my "Aha!" moment was to understand the message of eternity. The bank of eternity motto is, "You can't take it with you, but we can hold it until you get back." That means what we do to our earth, animals, trees and water affects us now and to eternity.

It's our planet; let us gently use it.

Terri Bowersock

THINK, BELIEVE, CREATE

Giorgio Tuscani

I was raised in a town with a population of 1,008—a town stricken with poverty and an attitude of resignation toward the situations and circumstances that were out of control. Agriculture was the only way to make a living. If you did not own the land, then you worked to harvest the crop.

I was around eight when Mom asked me if I wanted to go to Vacation Bible School. I remember thinking, "It's either Bible school or working in the fields," so, I asked her for her Bible. Mom never wanted me to work out in the fields, but I refused to see her alone and trying to make ends meet.

At bible school, our teacher read a parable from Scripture and asked us to draw whatever came to mind. When she saw my art, she said, "I know you will be a famous artist one day. This is a God-given talent."

Through the years, when I wasn't living with an aunt in one town or an uncle in another, things pretty much stayed the same. The church-hopping continued. The unsettling feeling that hopelessness and misery lay ahead of me was also a constant thought.

One summer, at the age of 17, I volunteered with my friends at their church. I was helping clean the pews when my friend turned to me and said, "Look at you trying to fit in. You will never belong." I literally froze, and a lump in my throat made it hard for me to swallow. Before my eyes welled up with tears, I handed him the towel and walked out.

I was tired of moving from place to place. I was tired of not being accepted—even by my own friends. I was tired of not knowing what was missing, or if anything was missing for that matter. I slowly began to resign to the fact that maybe this was the only way to live. "I'm not going to fight it anymore," I thought. "I'll just accept life as it is." Thoughts of suicide were constant. I moved from town to town finding jobs that lasted little more than a month. After a couple of years of sleeping on strangers' sofas I

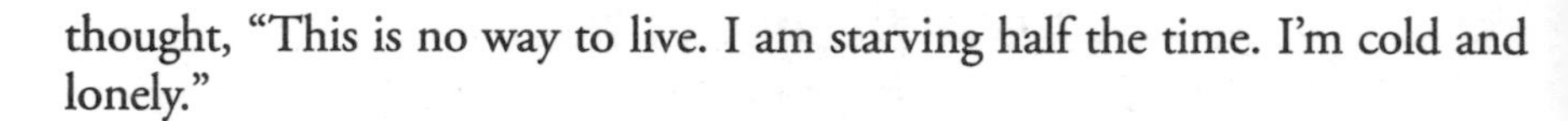

thought, "This is no way to live. I am starving half the time. I'm cold and lonely."

I had to end this miserable life. I began walking, and all the while I was cursing God and asking Him what I had done to deserve this. After hours of walking, I came across a park bench and sat down. I fell asleep and woke up the next morning shivering. Still angry and disgusted, I began thinking about how to commit suicide. Then I thought of my mom. What pain I would cause her. "She would just blame herself," I said. I could not bear to bring her pain. I thought about my Vacation Bible School teacher when I was eight. She not only believed in me, she knew I was going to be a famous artist. My mom was always encouraging and supportive as well. She believed in me. She said I could achieve and have anything I wanted if I just set my mind to it. My aunt told my mom I was the one who was going to make it in this life. I didn't know what she was talking about at the time. The more I thought about all the good things my mom, my aunt and my teacher had said, the better I felt. They must have known something that I didn't, but what?

I thought about what my friends told me throughout the years and how they treated me and how it angered me instantaneously. Then I thought about my mom and that made me smile. My mind was like a tennis match with those thoughts. I had good thoughts and bad thoughts; good people, bad people. Mom and Grandma were supportive and positive toward me. Some of my friends were pessimistic and negative. Then I thought about what Grandpa said: "Son, I'm too old to make waves. I'm okay with the way things are now. You have your whole life ahead of you. You are special. You are not going to be like the rest of us."

I was confused. How can Mom, Grandpa and Grandma be so supportive and knowingly believe I am going to make a difference, and yet not do that for themselves? They gave up on life and accepted whatever came their way—good or bad.

I kept going back to what Mom told me when I was a little kid and I came home crying because some of my friends told me I would not amount to anything because my uncles never amounted to anything. Mom held me and said, "Let's create a world where no one can hurt you, where you have all the toys you want, where you are happy." I was instantly smiling. "It does not matter what they think. I love you and believe in you with all my heart. What matters is what's in here." She pointed to my heart. "What you believe, what you think—that's what makes a difference." It hit me like a bolt of lightning. Think. Believe. Create. That was it. "Why can't I do that now?" I thought.

Thinking good thoughts is what turned my world around. Slowly but surely, my life got better. The Laws of Attraction were put into motion without my knowing.

The Laws of Attraction are like a mirror. The reflection is a situation or circumstance you create with your thoughts. A bad outcome is the cause of a negative thought. A happy outcome is created with a positive thought.

You must be consciously aware of your thoughts. These very thoughts create the situations and circumstances you find yourself in at every single moment. It does not cost anything to change your way of thinking, so think positive thoughts. Make them good, make them fun and make them last.

We are all artists. Our thoughts are paint brushes and tomorrow is a blank canvas. So let's start creating with our thoughts a beautiful painting for all to see and enjoy tomorrow!

Giorgio Tuscani

SOMETHING FROM NOTHING, WITH SOMETHING TO SHARE

Gregory Scott Reid

Betrayal: It can hit you like a load of bricks falling from the sky, leaving you with a feeling in the pit of your stomach no pill can cure. Starting your own business is hard enough. However, when your inside people are working against you, the toughest of souls can weaken at the knees.

Let me take you back a few years and share a little story with you. There I was, a fledgling in the corporate world. I had just quit my steady job and sold everything I had to venture out into entrepreneur life, when what I thought could never happen to me, happened. My closest friend and business partner wiped out our bank account balance, leaving me with debt up to my eyeballs and a lesson to be learned.

I believe that everything happens for a reason, so I pondered what the reason for my hardship could be. I was facing the biggest crossroad of my life. I had a failing business with no cash to save me, a close friend's betrayal and two roads heading in separate directions.

One road sent me after the person who had wronged me. I would obviously have a slam-dunk case and would win in any court. The other road had me using that same precious time and energy to focus in a more positive manner on rebuilding what I once had and learning from the experience. What would you do?

For myself, I chose the second of the two, knowing darned well that by wasting my thoughts and energy on revenge, there would be little time left to focus on what really mattered most: creating the business model and dream I had focused on in the first place.

What made me take this route, you ask? There is an old saying, "Many receive good advice, yet few actually profit from it." Since I chose to succeed, I went back and listened to all my old motivational tapes, thumbed through the books and messages and regained my focus. I quickly realized we are all dealt obstacles in this world.

There will always be stumbling blocks in our lives. That's just part of life. Our attitude toward these events shows the world who we are as individuals. It's been said that we learn more about someone on one bad day than on all his or her good days put together.

Have you ever wondered why some people seem to always have drama in their lives, while others simply go with the flow? Or why some people are happy and content most of the time, while others seem to attract only anger and chaos in their lives? I believe it's because what we feel and how we see ourselves on the inside is a direct reflection of how we feel and see the world around us. Someone once said to me, "We can't control our circumstances all the time, but we can control our attitudes toward them." I know that is a true statement, but, come on! I was stuck in a tight spot here!

So, there I was with a big decision to make. I decided to take on this challenge as just that: a challenge. If I could overcome this situation, which seemed so grave at the time and not only make it through it, but actually grow from it, then maybe my business partner didn't fail me after all.

Here's what I did: I moved on and buried the past. I went into the office the next day, changed the locks on the door, rolled up my sleeves and never looked back. It's amazing what a new coat of paint can do to a dreary old room. That's what I did for my business and my attitude toward it: out with the old and in with the new.

When I called all my customers and explained what had happened, you wouldn't believe the response. It was like a brotherhood of business people. Each person with whom I spoke had more advice than the last. It was strange that I had felt all alone and ashamed for letting someone take advantage of me, while others saw me as a new start up—simply green behind the ears. Remember, we all make mistakes.

There were many lessons learned that month. I took the advice given to me: I hired the best accounting person I could find as well as one of the best tax firms to oversee the accountant. Guess what happened? Business rose to record highs, allowing me to set my sights on growth rather than setbacks and to focus on the future rather than the past.

That was many, many years ago. The company became a corporation, and eventually the corporation was sold to another.

Now I find myself here, writing this story as if it were yesterday, remembering one of the greatest lessons I've learned.

In life, things will happen for the good and the bad. It's the way we handle these situations that makes us who we are.

It's all right to feel anger; it's okay to sense pain. In the end, when your story is written, which path will you have chosen? Live in the past, or live for the future.

Best wishes, and whatever you do...keep smilin'.

Gregory Scott Reid

STEP OUT OF THE SHADOW OF FEAR

David R. Hinson

It's 1985. I'm married with two children and another on the way. I'm chasing the American dream. My wife comes in from her neonatal visit and is visibly upset. There is a potential problem with the pregnancy.

I always believed that things happen for a reason and the challenges of life can be overcome through prayer and the belief that good will always prevail over evil. These were a part of the fundamental teachings within my church, but my family was in danger. I feared for my wife and our unborn child.

I feared that if we terminated the pregnancy, our union could be considered a failure. We discussed this, prayed over it and decided we would move forward with the pregnancy.

We were determined to give our unborn child a chance at life. We recognized the potential outcomes—she could be stillborn or she could be born with any number of maladies—but we wanted to try. You see, our other two children were not my natural children. They were hers from a previous relationship. I had carried a degree of doubt that I could even make children. So I decided when I married, I would marry a woman with children and love them like they were my own, and I did just that.

We moved forward in our decision to have our baby and revel in the joy of our union. So, the big day arrived. The doctors thought it would be best to deliver by Cesarean section, and on June 26, at 10:00 a.m., we welcomed our daughter into the world. I watched the entire procedure. This was one of the proudest and most victorious moments of my life. We had beaten the odds!

We made it through that hurdle, but there was more to consider. How healthy was our newborn child? How was my wife doing? These questions would be answered with time. Everyone was miraculously fine. We closed out the year on a truly joyous and appreciative note, with thoughts and expectations of better days ahead.

The following year was great. We took the kids on vacation and celebrated the first year of our baby's life. My wife was physically stronger and was considering going back to work. Life was vibrant and joyful. Summer drifted into fall and fall into winter—then it happened.

My wife came home complaining that she felt weak. She was having difficulty eating; there were moments when breathing became problematic. We went to the hospital and the doctor's prognosis was optimistic. But, as we closed in on the second week of hospitalization, my wife took a turn for the worse. She had trouble breathing and required a tube, leaving her unable to speak, so I brought her a notebook so she could share her thoughts and feelings.

During her third week, my wife wrote in her notebook, "Don't break up our family." I wondered what she meant. Why would she say something like that? She floored me with the real possibility that she might not come back home with me. She said she would be going home soon. I always understood that to mean that she was coming home with me and the kids, but this was clearly a different message.

I was in denial. We'd just survived the first ordeal with her and the baby and we thought we were out of the woods. This was a significant challenge, but not an insurmountable one. I needed to deal with this as we had with the first challenge: believe, have faith and pray. I left work early that Friday around 1:00 so I could have more time with my wife. I wasn't prepared for what awaited as I made my way down the corridor where she was staying.

A doctor approached me to discuss my wife's condition. "She went into cardiac arrest," he stated. They had had a very difficult time resuscitating, and she had experienced oxygen deprivation. She was stabilizing, but her

prognosis was not good. "What is oxygen deprivation?" I asked. The doctor told me it is a situation in which the brain is without oxygen for a period of time. "How much time?" I asked quietly. "Eight to ten minutes," he replied. "She is in a coma currently, and we don't know whether she will ever come out of it." The doctor indicated that my wife could go in to cardiac arrest at any time, and I should consider a "do not resuscitate" authorization.

Soon, the doctor came back with more discouraging news. My wife had very little brain activity. They were not resolute in saying she was brain dead, but they strongly suggested she wasn't far from it. Since she was on a ventilator, they thought we should consider disconnecting it and let her expire naturally.

What a day. My ailing wife took a turn for the worst and lay in a virtual dead zone. The doctors had done all they could and wanted me to consider unplugging the only lifeline she had. I stayed with her that night, returned Saturday mid-morning and prayed early Sunday morning. I had planned to go back to the hospital around noon.

I had not authorized the "do not resuscitate" directive. I wasn't going to pull the plug, deciding to leave it in God's hands. As I got ready to leave for the hospital, the telephone rang. My mother answered, and with a blank, sobering stare, she said, "She's gone home." I had to hurry to the hospital. I couldn't accept this. What were the kids and I going to do?

When I arrived at the hospital, the nurses had cleaned up my wife and allowed me some time with her before moving her to the morgue. It was a surreal moment. My wife looked so normal, and it almost seemed, at times, as if she was breathing. I wanted so much to believe that she was, but when I touched her hand, reality came rushing back: she was gone. My wife was dead. There was nothing left for me to do, and I had a more daunting job—I needed to tell the older children that Mommy was not coming home: ever.

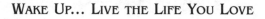

We got through the funeral while the dust of the tragedy was still settling and the reality of moving forward was beginning. I was in my mid-twenties with three children; my in-laws wanted the children and my mother wanted the children, but I promised not to break up our family. I decided to keep my family together and make it work!

Now, 20 years later, my little girl is in college, pursuing her dream to become a lawyer. My older daughter works in the pharmaceutical industry as a contract manager, and my son—the oldest—is building his own contracting business. I am working in the public sector and operating several home-based businesses. I have a property acquisition company and a life coaching and business development firm. I have used my experiences, challenges and obstacles to create opportunity. I have learned that prayer and the power of determined belief are pathways to success. I have confronted my own personal challenges and I've raised fully capable and successful children who utilize their experiences to build and expand their lives. Define the purpose for your life and overcome your fears. I did it, and you can too!

David R. Hinson

DON'T GET MAD... GET GORGEOUS!

Rayeleen Gilbert

The road ahead was a blur, as tears welled up in her eyes. Her jaw clenched and her breathing quickened while her body tensed. Her hands gripped tighter on the steering wheel as the anger began to rise again, like a bubbling volcano. Her sweet, youthful, 23-year-old face and innocent smile were taking cover behind an angry mask, giving her a false sense of security. Real or not, any security would do.

The memory replayed in her mind like a horror movie, consuming her, pushing her back into the seat of the car. The memory created repulsive feelings in her body again—she held back the desire to vomit as the feelings intensified.

"Why don't they just go away?" she screamed. These thoughts, these memories, were triggered by men who looked at her, by any sexual innuendo, by people in authority—by men in general.

She was exhausted from constantly fighting with a desire to see these men disappear from the planet. She wanted them to pay for what they had done. She was consumed by thoughts of hatred and revenge. She was victimized by her own mind—by her own thoughts.

Then, suddenly, there was stillness. Silence. An unexplainable reverence filled the air. A large book appeared in front of her and opened. Then a voice like no other voice she had ever heard before spoke in strong, commanding, words. It was everywhere and nowhere all at once, and it pressed lovingly into every cell of her being:

"Rayeleen, sweet child, every time you think of him—of them—you spend time with them, and they do not deserve your love. When you read a book, the pages flickering backwards, do not keep going over all of the old chapters. Tear them up and throw them away. Every thought you have creates your very next

moment. Don't get mad; get as gorgeous as you can be. Outshine them. Outshine them all. Whenever a thought of them is triggered, use it as fuel to surge forward on your journey to happiness. You can create whatever you want. The fairy tale begins with your thoughts. And, you can even re-write the old chapters if you want. You can re-write them however you choose. Your truth is yours alone and survives only by your thoughts. Take your mind away from anything and it will dissolve. Your truth, your reality, is only ever a product of your thoughts. That is all it is. Without thought, they do not exist. You are the creator. You create your thoughts. Choose carefully."

She sat in stunned silence, her hands still on the steering wheel. She was unable to explain what had just happened, but somehow she understood. Her body relaxed, her breathing soft and calm. A warm glow embraced her and a feeling of joyful excitement had replaced the nausea. Tears of relief and release traced her cheeks and glistened in the moonlight. I was never the same.

I wanted to shout to the world, "I am happy! I am free! Free to be me!" From that day forward, everything changed for me. By choice, I became free of those old, tormenting thoughts. I left the past behind me.

No matter what happens in my life today, it does not disturb my inner serenity. I choose happiness. Because of this, many people ask me if I ever experience challenges and difficulties in my own life. Of course I do. I am human. I get angry, sad and hurt. I am a mother to three teenagers, a stepmother to another three teenagers, and a nanny to a 2-year-old. I am a wife, a friend, a daughter, a sister and a businesswoman. I live in the world. However, nothing is permitted to hold on to me for too long. I quickly and intentionally return to a place of joy.

I have unwavering faith in the power of love. I believe the answer to every question is love. I believe in a greater power, and to me, that greater power is love. I see difficulties and problems as challenges whereby I get to experience more of who I am and who I am not. My intention is to become more loving with every breath, thought, word and action, and I definitely get to practice! I get to practice what I have learned and what I teach. After all, this is a spiritual practice. An absence of problems is not enlightenment—it is an absence of life!

Helen Keller said, "You could never learn to be brave and patient if there were only joy in the world." Someone was looking out for me. It could have been my own wisdom, a guardian angel or a spirit guide. I don't know for certain and it does not matter. I know there is a divine plan. Each one of us is a very important part of that plan and the world would not be the same without one of us. I had a choice. I had the ability to create my own fairytale and that's what I did.

Today I am living the fairytale of my life and I have no doubt we can be and have whatever we want. We are the artists of our own lives and we should paint the most beautiful pictures we can imagine. Every thought is a brushstroke on that canvas. We can paint whatever we wish, and we can paint out whatever we don't want. We are that powerful.

Begin today. Decide to paint a masterpiece with your thoughts, and a masterpiece is what you shall have. You are unique in this gallery of life. You deserve your place and you are priceless.

Rayeleen Gilbert

THE BLINK OF AN EYE

Judy Strong

On January 8, 1991, my husband died. In the blink of an eye, I became a widow, a single parent and a bread winner. Grief and fear seized me as I thought of our three children still living at home. I knew I had my work cut out for me.

Our lives had been those typical of middle class families. My husband was a successful salesman, I worked part-time as an early childhood teacher, and our children were growing up nicely and finding their own paths in life. Our oldest daughter was already pursuing her career in another state.

My husband suffered with rheumatoid arthritis since his late twenties. This is a painful and crippling disease that we coped with daily. As it progressed, the crippling increased, resulting in a diminished capacity to function. There was uncertainty and insecurity for us all, but determination and a positive attitude fired our spirits. Even when he began to have replacement surgery for worn joints, we geared up and put our best foot forward. I truly believed life would get better, and we would grow old together.

I was 50 when my husband died. The children were 25, 20, 17 and 15. We had life insurance, a 401k, and some investments, which we planned to use for our retirement. I was reluctant to dip too deeply into my resources, but my salary was inadequate, and I knew I needed a better paying job. That blink of an eye completely turned my life around. I went from being a homemaker with a part-time job and growing family to full-time employee and college student. Needing just a few credits to complete my degree, I decided to dig in and graduate.

Making ends meet wasn't the only obstacle I faced. Binding up wounds was a major, ongoing task. Our emotional well-being was paramount, and I prioritized its importance, both short- and long-term.

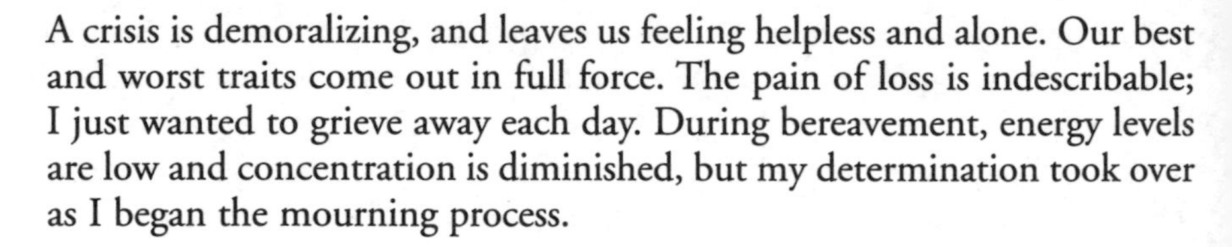

A crisis is demoralizing, and leaves us feeling helpless and alone. Our best and worst traits come out in full force. The pain of loss is indescribable; I just wanted to grieve away each day. During bereavement, energy levels are low and concentration is diminished, but my determination took over as I began the mourning process.

Mourning isn't sitting still. Grief is work and as I faced each obstacle and solved each problem, I again felt my spirit fire up. I sought help when I needed it and always found people around me–sometimes professionals, sometimes friends or neighbors–who had the insight I lacked. I realized we could live with some uncertainty, as long as we took comfort in one another's love and warmth. We embraced hope and reaffirmed that positive attitude that had sustained our family while we dealt with illness and disability.

Today, I am confident and self-sufficient. My children are mature and independent, and we are amazed at the hurdles we jumped. Fear and dread have been replaced with joy and an unshakable sense of belonging to one another. The family is scattered all over the map, but each Christmas we celebrate at my house in Arizona. No one wants to miss it, because it's the only time we can all be together.

Not long ago, I met someone who brought love into my life again, and we were married. The extended family is added pleasure, and, together, we have six grandchildren to spoil. It doesn't get any better than that!

My wish for you is to have that same joy and sense of peace that comes from living each day—not as a challenge—but as a gift. Start to build a foundation today, wherever you may be on your life path. Resources abound, within and around you. Look inside, affirm yourself and tap into it. Trust your own instincts.

Share your bounty with those in need. Wrap your arms around them and give freely. If we wait until we think we have abundance to give, the fire in our spirit will begin to go out. The foundation you build and share will spread throughout the community, and there will be abundant resources to sustain everyone.

The blink of an eye that pushed me into a new life seemed instantaneous, but was really part of an ongoing process I hadn't recognized. My coping skills were already in place, and my emotional content lay dormant, to be summoned when crisis struck. Your foundation touches every aspect of your being—mental, emotional, physical and spiritual. Build it carefully and consistently. Let others help you and believe, if you wish, that the Creator Spirit is pouring out love and joy.

I remember the pain and anxiety of those first few years of widowhood. The responsibility was overwhelming, and I would sit at the kitchen table and think, "When do they let you cry?" Now I know that you have to let the tears flow. It clears your head and soothes your soul. In the blink of an eye, I moved from reasonable comfort to what seemed an insurmountable task. But here I am, still designing my new life. My late husband believed life was meant to be enjoyed, not endured. My wake-up moment handed that legacy to me. I live by it, and I encourage you to do the same. I wish you well.

Judy Strong

RELEASING YOUR BRAKES

Brian Tracy

Do you have any ideas or attitudes about yourself and your abilities that may be holding you back from great success and happiness? As it happens, everyone does.

In her wonderful book, *You Can Heal Your Life*, Louise Hay says each one of us has feelings of inferiority that are manifested in the conclusion that we are not good enough. We think we are not as good as other people, and we feel we are not good enough to acquire and enjoy the things we want in life. Very often, we feel we don't deserve good things. Even if we do work hard and achieve some worthwhile objectives, we believe that we are not really entitled to our successes, and we often engage in behaviors that sabotage them. The fact is that you deserve every good thing you are capable of acquiring as the result of your talents.

You must develop your beliefs about yourself to the point where they serve you every day, in every way. Men and women who accomplish extraordinary things are just ordinary people who have mentally developed themselves enough to overcome the obstacles that stood in their way. They kept on keeping on until their goal was attained.

The most harmful beliefs you can have are what are called "self-limiting beliefs." These are mostly untrue beliefs about yourself, but they hold you back nonetheless. Sometimes you—or those around you—will say you cannot achieve certain goals because you do not have enough education. The humorist Josh Billings once said, "It ain't what a man knows what hurts him. It's what a man knows what ain't true." It isn't the actual truth about yourself and your abilities that hurts you; it's the things you consider to be true.

The starting point of changing your ideas is to muster up the courage to question them seriously. Question your basic beliefs. Check your assumptions. Ask yourself, "What assumptions am I making about myself or my situation that might not be true?" It's a fact that we fall in love with our excuses and our negative assumptions. We fall in love with our reasons for not moving ahead.

The author Richard Bach wrote, "Argue for your limitations, and sure enough, they're yours." Very often, we become the prosecuting attorney in the case against ourselves. We dispute and argue and attempt to prove to ourselves and to others that our limitations are real, and the less justification these ideas or beliefs have, the more adamant we become in attempting to prove them to others.

Whatever your limitations, resolve to challenge them. Hold them up to the light. Imagine you had absolute confidence in yourself in a particular area. Then, act as if it were impossible to fail, and so shall it be!

Here are three steps you can take immediately to put these ideas into action:

- First, accept that you are as good and as talented in your own way as anyone else you will ever meet. There is nothing you can't accomplish if you really want it.

- Second, challenge a belief or idea you have about yourself that is holding you back. What if you had an extraordinary ability in that area? What difference would it make in your life?

- Third, stop making excuses for your lack of success. Instead, start making progress. Think and talk about what you want and then get busy making it come true.

Brian Tracy

LIFE'S TOO SHORT

Joanne Rainey

In 1997, I was just your average American woman. My background was typical lower middle class, and I was one of three daughters of a single mom. My early success in life consisted of being the first one in the family to get a college degree, getting married, having two wonderful children and staying home to raise them. My life was indistinguishable from most people in my circle of friends and family. I did not spend time wondering if I was happy or if I was living the life I wanted. Like most people, I just woke up every day, took care of my loved ones, did my daily chores and put my dreams on hold for "some day," when I would have the time and the luxury to really think about what I wanted. "Some day" always existed far in the future somewhere, and I lived with mild discomfort and expectancy waiting for that day to arrive. In an unlimited future, there is always tomorrow.

All of us will experience the opportunity for transitional moments in our lives, whether we choose to notice them or not. Some of them will come in with subtle quietness, and we must pay attention to recognize them. Some of them will come in with loud, thunderous noise, impossible to ignore. If we are lucky, we will receive the subtle, not so painful opportunities. If we are not so lucky, we may receive earsplitting thunder that will knock us to the floor and require months or even years for us to recover. My thunderous moment began in a hospital late on a Friday night in May.

Like most parents today, my children are the largest and best part of my life. My son, Jack, was seven years old and my daughter, Natalia, had just turned four. Natalia had been showing vague symptoms that she was not well, and after several doctor visits, we finally insisted she have some tests done at the Children's Hospital. The first day she was there, more and more doctors went in and out of her room. By the end of the day, we had the diagnosis every parent dreads: cancer. When your child is diagnosed

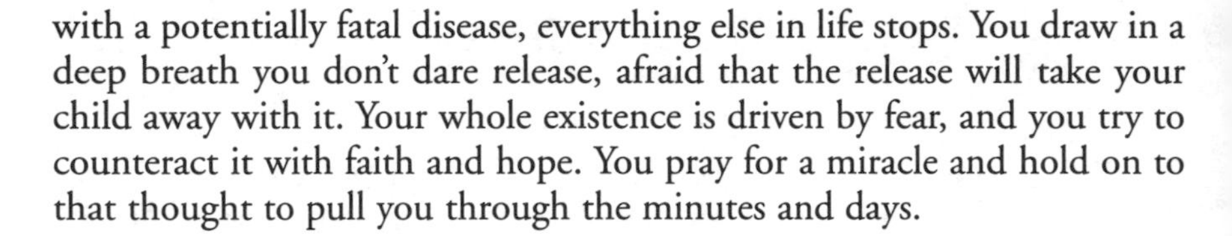

with a potentially fatal disease, everything else in life stops. You draw in a deep breath you don't dare release, afraid that the release will take your child away with it. Your whole existence is driven by fear, and you try to counteract it with faith and hope. You pray for a miracle and hold on to that thought to pull you through the minutes and days.

Natalia died on June 13th, 1997–two weeks after she was admitted to the hospital and three days before my 36th birthday. The breath was released, and there was only darkness. My whole focus became just getting through the next moment. I reached out to the only lifeline I could find and my reason to survive: my son, Jack. I made myself a promise that I would not allow his childhood to be ruined by his sister's death, that we would not only survive this experience but that life would be good again someday. I went back to work to create mental distraction, and I threw myself into trying to understand how to navigate this new world called grief. I just kept moving, hoping my broken heart would remember how to beat.

Extreme grief often brings a fierce clarity of purpose. The questions I never bothered to ask myself (or left unanswered if they did cross my mind) became the focus of my thoughts: "Why am I here, what is my path, how do I survive this darkness and what do I do with the experience to acquire more positive energy? How do I survive this tragedy and still have a life worth living?" I began to explore areas of my spirituality I had never known even existed. The search for peace, mentally and spiritually, became my journey. I slowly removed negativity and passiveness from my life and replaced it with positive thinking and behaviors.

One of the most important questions I asked myself was, "Is the life I am living the one I wanted or was it a life based on fear? Fear of losing something, not succeeding, losing control or fear of emotional pain?" I understood that I had been challenged with the largest fear a person can face, and I was surviving. Never again would I let fear stop me from doing the things I wanted to do. I asked myself the very difficult question, "What do I really want?" How could I exit the darkness and start entering into the light? The answers started to come, and with them came hope. I now fearlessly choose to do something based on whether it fits my life plan and what I want.

Five years after the loss of my daughter, I finally started to live again. I realized my life would need to be very different from what I had always known. I quit my nice but unsatisfying corporate job and started my own company. My old life experiences and beliefs started falling to the side, and I incorporated new spiritual direction into my life. I began to write and was published several times, even internationally. I finally got out of my own way and started to live the life I now knew I wanted. This change was sometimes uncomfortable for myself and those around me, as I challenged myself to clearly identify my purpose in life and to allow into my life only the actions, people and experiences that would drive me toward my purpose.

The phrase, "Life's too short" is no longer a flippant sentiment; it became my reality. We can choose to live a life of purpose or we can choose to sleepwalk through our life, whether it is four years or 100 years long. We can choose to be engaged or to be asleep. I chose to Wake Up and Live!

Joanne Rainey

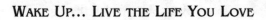

PURPOSE

Sabrina-Marie Wilson

Many times, the pain you are running from is your purpose or assignment in this lifetime. It is staring you in the face, and you are still running until it confronts you and you have nowhere to hide.

On a very chilly winter day, while walking to school, thoughts of my life's purpose were heavy on my heart. With tears in my eyes, I marched down the hill as the cold air burned in my chest. I considered it an accomplishment simply to get to school because I was often out of breath before my first period class. My life at that point consisted of ongoing doctor appointments, lab work, treatments, medical procedures and hospitalizations. The routine was painful, scary and uncertain because I didn't know if my health would allow me to continue to enjoy being a teenager. At the same time, I feared letting my peers get close enough to know about what I was going through. The few that did know thought I was lying and just teased me about my frail appearance. I was a five-foot three-inch, 85-pound freshman.

I was born with several physical conditions, including a genetic blood disease called Cooley's anemia. From early childhood to my teens, my weak physical health made my daily routine uncertain. As the years progressed, the quality of my physical health declined. It affected my class attendance, concentration and ability to continue much-loved activities such as dance, girl scouts, sports and band. I also lost some childhood peers to this disease.

I was an Army brat and had several chores and responsibilities as a kid. They helped me to become a forward thinker and to persist in meeting my goals. I kept busy with a few extra-curricular activities when I could. Reading and studying everything from alternative healthcare and nutrition to fashion and style techniques helped improve my physical appearance and stamina. In addition, I read my Bible. I studied the people in the chapters to find spiritual comfort and as a way to escape. Before long,

I met other teens who had an interest in fashion and drama. They became a support system for me. Still, I always wondered how I would ever contribute to society.

I went to college with a desire to serve society by helping my community and improving human rights. I saw it as fun way to meet terrific people, learn from others and help others. I consistently saw my parents do this throughout my childhood. Once or twice a month I volunteered at battered women's shelters and soup kitchens, spoke to support groups, and brought others with me. Then I reached out to convince the friends I met at hospitals and support groups to join me. I learned that people can inspire you with their presence, grace and strength no matter what their situation or ability.

In my personal Scripture studies, one verse jumped out of the Bible and pierced my soul. *"Man looks upon the outer appearances, but God looks upon the heart."* (1 Samuel 16:7)

HEART

The attitude of the heart sets the tone for everything we do. The first thing people see is our appearance, and if they see a person with a health challenge, many times they do not even consider that person's abilities, talents or heart. In prayer time, these words came to my mind:

Helping to **E**ncourage **A**bilities and **R**ecognizing **T**alents

One day, during my treatment at the hospital, I was approached by a lady who noticed I was speaking to a group of patients at a clinic. She wanted to know what I was doing. After explaining my project and my status as an undergraduate student, she identified herself as a college career counselor. This contact sent me to yet another advisor and an exciting new direction in my life, a direction that made me publicly face what I had been running from: myself.

I was invited to a university research center by the director, a national leader in the area of employment and disability rights and a current U.S. presidential appointee. She became my college mentor. My own personal life experiences, volunteer and community work enhanced my research center work.

My training focused on everyday socioeconomic issues impacting the lives of millions. These issues included gainful employment, maintaining quality healthcare, and accessible and affordable housing and transportation. I also attended legislative forum days on Capitol Hill that addressed these issues.

During this time, I was able to meet and learn from top leaders in this field, including many living with physical challenges. Their various professions inspire and challenge me to reach for even higher goals. In addition, I met national civil rights icons and worked on events honoring historical civil rights milestones of our time.

When I look back on my early years of pain and uncertainty, I am grateful. I see many blessings in the things that did not fall perfectly into place in my life and in some of the social rejection I received as a kid. These lessons encouraged me to search for a better place. It challenged me to carve out my own niche.

The most important lesson I have learned is that time and people are very precious gifts. In less than a few years, many of the mentors who confronted me with awesome learning experiences have passed on, and I honor them by pressing ahead to new opportunities to help many generations.

Sabrina-Marie Wilson

REALIZING TRUE IMPORTANCE
Aaron Silverman

My wake up moment came when one of my best friends passed on. Twenty-five is much too young to leave this world, and his passing sent me down a path that led me to where I am today. These are a few simple truths I learned from my friend and the way he lived his life.

What is most important in life? It's simple: family and friends. Period. He may not have kept in touch with everyone as much as he might have, but he was always thinking of them. The Tuesday before his accident, a group of us went to a hockey game. We reminisced about the good old days, and you would not believe the number of people and the good times we recalled. We even talked about friends we had not seen or heard from in years. My friend lived his life with as few regrets as possible; however, I know one of his greatest regrets was not staying in touch with people as much as he wished.

Do my friend a favor—pick up the phone or open your email and say a quick hello to all of those people you have not been contacting. You keep saying you will call them next week, but next week never seems to come.

What is really important? To my friend, it was simple—relax, slow down and enjoy life. My friend loved his job and dedicated extra time to it, but he also knew how to have fun. He had a great balance between work and life. Too many of us forget work is not life. If it did not involve family, friends or enjoying life, it was not important to him at all, and after a bit of reflecting, I tend to agree.

After the funeral, I decided to follow his lead and started living life. I went completely out of my comfort zone and took a risk. I took a job in Kuwait as an environmental contractor working for the U.S. Army. I had no idea what was in store for me, but I knew I wanted to live abroad for a year and travel.

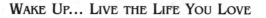

For a while, life was good. I enjoyed my job. I made some great friends, and I experienced a completely different culture. I traveled a lot in one year. I celebrated New Year's in Bahrain, rode a camel to the pyramids in Giza, did some shopping in Dubai, backpacked through Germany during the World Cup (cheering like a crazy man at all three USA matches), flew halfway around the world for a friend's wedding, flew a plane, jumped out of a plane and the list goes on and on.

As I said, life was good, but then I got promoted. Life was even better—or so I thought. With the promotion, I threw out my plan to only stay on the job for one year. I signed up for one more year to see how things went. I lost track of my plan to experience the world and then go home.

I quickly learned the burden of middle management and the joys of responsibility without the authority to adequately manage them. My stress-free, enjoy-life-and-go-with-the-flow lifestyle went out the window somewhere along the way as the reality of the new job set in.

I became testy and constantly stressed at work. It did not take long for the stress and anxiety to spill over from work to the rest of my life. I lost track of what my friend's life taught me, and I did not even realize it.

I was unhappy, and knew something had to change. But I was not sure what or how. Yom Kipper was coming up in a few days, and I decided there was no better day to reflect than the day built into my religion for that purpose. I told my boss I was not coming to work that day, and I stayed home. I do not follow all of the Jewish holidays as I should; however, something had to change, and that something was me.

I am not sure if it was the day of reflecting or the 23 hours without food and water, but about an hour before sunset, I made my decision: I was leaving Kuwait and moving home. I realized family and friends were all that mattered, and after 16 months in Kuwait, it was time to go home.

At that moment my stress disappeared. I had no idea what I was going to do when I got home, but that did not matter. On my way home, I started living my life again. I picked up on my traveling habits and stopped in London for a few days to visit some friends, and I surprised some family in Boston before I arrived home.

It has been over a year since I left Kuwait, and I have been self-employed since then (or as I like to say, successfully unemployed). Since I have been home, I traveled a bit more, started to find lost friends and continued to live my life as I wanted to live.

Whether you realize it or not, you learn a little something from every interaction. Some of what you learn will be good and some will be bad; however, it is how you apply what you gained that will determine if you had a positive or negative experience. My friend's passing taught me that.

Since the tragic event sent me down an unexpected road, my small world has been opened to a larger and richer one.

Aaron Silverman

AWARENESS CREATES CLARITY ON THE PATH TO SUCCESS

Axel Meierhoefer

I was allowed to protect the skies over Europe and the United States for 20 years without having to eject from a fighter jet—a great achievement in my mind. Having the opportunity to teach others how to do it was an equally fulfilling assignment.

I was entrusted with a leading role in managing the largest foreign development project ever completed by the German military. It allowed me to efficiently move towards the opening day, doing all the right things to achieve the goals of the Air Force leadership. We found a way to add effectiveness to the mix by integrating more than 500 computers, when 50 might have been expected. Looking back, I feel proud.

After retiring and working for a software company, leading a growing team of trainers and customer service providers was gratifying and shed light on the differences between the military and a corporate environment. Becoming my own boss and developing my company into a successful enterprise started as a scary endeavor and remains a daily challenge.

Through all these important events and steps of my life, you would think a wake-up moment would have occurred at some point along the way. In reality, it hadn't. Yet, often when things looked grim and the skies were obscured by clouds of doubt, problems and seemingly insurmountable obstacles, I found a way to succeed.

The wake up moment that brought clarity wasn't really one single event or realization, but the culmination of three elements woven together.

- The first part was the movement sparked by the movie, "The Secret" and its message of energy, connectedness, and the Law of Attraction.

- The second part was my completion of a performance assessment test and the associated certification training which identified me as a master level performer and gave data to support this claim. This is when I finally realized I had the basic ingredients for success.

- The third part, and probably the most important one, was recognizing that the combination of trust, passion and positive energy bring the people and circumstances into my life that allow me to be successful.

The wake-up moment occurred for me when I began trusting myself to use all I have learned to serve others. This service is aimed at helping them help themselves to become successful.

With the combination of trust, love from and for my wife and daughter, positive energy and the determination to pass on what I have learned, what I once considered work is now the passionate pursuit of happiness. It allows me to attract individuals into my life who will be an inspiration for the things to come. I can fully enjoy the praise I receive from people for whom I help to find solutions, or from those I life-coach.

This means empowering those I come in contact with to be passionate and help them find their passion. Instead of allowing them to be depressed, self-critical, skeptical or downright unmotivated by what seems to be the burden of life, I offer a positive message and encouragement to search for a passion and then pursue it.

When the passion has been identified, or at least a notion of what it could be is visible, I try to be the coach and motivator who urges his friends, customers and clients to take action in the direction of their goal or passion. When people tell me that they need to figure out what the right action is, I push them to take any action that moves them forward. They gain confidence, discover their ambitions and enjoy the new relationships that form. They literally attract what they need, just as I do in my work.

Not every step is perfectly correct, and sometimes people make mistakes.

I have learned not to be afraid of mistakes, but to look at them as risks that bear the potential for success. When a mistake ultimately happens, my associates and I accept it and learn from it. It will increase the awareness needed to overcome obstacles, which is half of the solution. Mistakes help us on our path to mastery and wisdom.

I have learned that the sum of knowledge and experience leads to wisdom while the sum of skill and experience leads to mastery. The former is based more on mind power; the latter on our natural talents and skills. While taking steps towards these two goals, mistakes cannot be avoided. Discovering them early and learning from them is what feeds our experience.

Naturally, it would be easy to lecture others about these things. More importantly, I am trying to be a role model and lead others to success. I enjoy being trusted and asked for suggestions and help. What I discover, I pass on. Sometimes it makes me a profit or gets me closer to my goals. More often than not, it helps me over a roadblock or obstacle or it serves as a solution to a problem.

Since I have experienced the three elements of my wake up moment, I enjoy each case where my help and services have changed the lives of students and coachees in a way that caused them to believe in their great, positive and wonderful futures.

In a nutshell, I gained the clarity of awareness to realize I can walk on the clouds of contribution and enjoy the soulful sunshine of service, achieving my goals while helping others achieve theirs. Positive energy and passionate guides surrounding me will allow me to be a miracle worker and spread joy throughout the world.

I invite everyone to join me on this journey towards success, becoming wise and achieving mastery through passionate action with the benefit of others in mind.

Axel Meierhoefer

THE EDGE

Dr. John G. Bickert

Manfred bumps past his siblings, reaching for the extra morsel. He flips over the nest brim and plummets. Dread fills his being, but a strange sense of belonging mitigates the horror. The eternal fall ends abruptly with a crushing thud. Manfred lies face down, sore and confused. He struggles to his wobbly legs and staggers. Pain paralyzes his side. Sick with fear, the young bird gazes up to the nest. It is a small, dark blip hardly visible in the canopy above.

"I'll never get back!" he laments.

Night descends as Manfred rests motionlessly, waiting to be rescued. He raises his head from the frost-laden ground, and perceives blurred moonbeam remnants touching down in silver patches. The security and boldness that made him the dominant eaglet is nothing more than a dream. How can he regain what he once possessed? He raises both wings, and with as much force as he can muster, draws an arc in imitation of his majestic mother. A clawing pain strikes his right side. He quickly tucks his wings and notices the right one does not hug his side as neatly as it had. Immediately, his bold resolution is squashed. He abandons flight, seeing it as impossible. Manfred sinks beneath the tree and lets a loud, solitary screech labor from his mouth. The consequence of bad luck and poor judgment thrusts Manfred into despair. He lowers his sore head and neck to his left wing and submits with a painful breath. Arching his neck, he cries once again. This time a fog plume rises toward the full moon. The night is cold on the forest floor and Manfred releases periodic cries to the stars. He sees looming arms of trees stretching forth their limbs in celebration of victory over him.

"What a wretch!" he whimpers in self-regret. "What a dismal failure."

The haunting forest sounds are broken by calm, rhythmic wing beats. An owl settles on a branch and emits a mocking, vacant, "Whoooo!"

Distraught, Manfred looks up and sees the moon partially obscure a clear view of the perched visitor.

"So, who are you?" he inquires. "Forget it. You can't help me."

Looking for a reaction, he moves his head from side to side to gain a better view. He positions the owl's silhouette so as to fully eclipse the bright moon. Manfred first sees the bird's dark, backlit image and strains to see its face.

Without turning his body, as if mocking Manfred's stiff neck, the owl looks back at the moon and then turns to Manfred.

"Ken Nestor," says the owl. "Why so glum?"

"I fell from my nest."

"Oh, I thought it was something serious," the owl returns. "Just fly back."

"Just as I thought—a philosophizing Minerva with magical solutions," mocks Manfred.

"What are the wings for?"

Chafed, Manfred reveals his despair in a mocking tone, "As if."

"The average person's tolerance for failure is once," Ken says. "You lack one thing."

"What's that?" Manfred asks hopefully. "Can this mythical Cheshire actually help?"

The owl drops a one-word response, "Nope!"

"Nope? What's that mean?" Manfred asks, exasperated.

"You don't have it," says Ken.

"What?" Manfred screams.

"Get a grip! Right now, you don't have everything required to be successful."

Manfred remembers the displaced feathers. "Perhaps Ken is right! Why didn't I think of that? I need to be well-plumed. Adornment is everything," he thinks. Manfred resolves to be groomed in the morning. Excitement wells and he can hardly wait.

The next morning, Manfred excitedly reflects on his mother's frequent visits to the orniaesthetician. He sits still for feather grooming, bill honing and talon trimming. Later, feeling like new, he presents himself to Ken for validation. That evening, Ken arrives as he had the previous night, but is unenthusiastic.

"Well, it's an improvement, but you're still missing something," Ken says, peering at the moon.

"What?" Manfred asks in alarm. A thought pierces his brain and he bolts upright. "Aviation ground school! That's it! I wish I'd thought of that earlier! That's the key! Limited education is probably the one significant drawback blocking future success," he reasons.

Manfred attends the local Orniflight School. He studies hard to learn flight intricacies. Theories, ordinances, weights, balances, lift and drag preoccupy him. He finishes with good marks and joyfully welcomes graduation. Manfred is anxious to see Ken with his newly upgraded education.

Ken seems unimpressed. "Humph, you think that'll get you to the nest?

You still don't have it."

"My heavens, what's missing?" inquires Manfred in disbelief.

Ken does not respond and turns his face to the moon.

Manfred is beside himself. He screams at the top of his lungs, "What do they expect?" He places his head beneath his wing and weeps.

"Stop that! What do you think that'll accomplish?" says Ken, turning back. "You're acting like an immature human. Stop feeling sorry for yourself. I'm not the least bit impressed by your emotional outbursts!"

Manfred becomes despondent. He turns his negative gaze inward. Ken Nestor tires of his depressed friend's complaining spirit and stops the nightly visits. The flightless eagle no longer believes he will return to the nest. At best, all Manfred can muster are short bursts of flight, similar to a barnyard hen. When flying, he panics and flops and flips like a drowning swimmer. Manfred looks up at his siblings soaring above. Having given up, he hides from others and is seldom seen above the lowest levels of the forest.

Ken returns weeks later to Manfred's surprise. Deeply ashamed, Manfred crouches to hide but is unsuccessful. A cloud hides the bright moon and darkness descends like a deep frost.

Almost imperceptibly, Ken admonishes, "I see you still haven't got it. It looks like you've gained weight and become quite content to spend your life among squirrels, gophers, worms and snakes."

"I can't fly! I've tried. I just can't get up. I don't know what's wrong. I guess I'm not made to fly," Manfred says.

"You're an eagle. You're made to soar. You just refuse to accept the one missing element." Ken pauses, turns in the direction of the moon as if it is a source of wisdom. He turns back. "Unfortunately, you don't have that slight edge to make you a winner."

"You're playing games. I'm past the point of wanting nebulous advice. I followed your advice in the past and look where I am. Nowhere!" Manfred scolds.

Ken laughs, "I'm happy to see you still have life after all."

From the darkness, Ken's voice penetrates with clearness, "What you really need is the credibility edge. Success will not come from flapping your wings a few times in all directions. Relax and focus on your goal. Don't focus on yourself. Stay tuned to the objective and don't be distracted. The credibility edge will come when your confidence grows and you trust your talents."

A barely perceptible snap occurs deep in Manfred's brain, like a spirit of oppression had been lifted. It is small, but cannot be ignored. A strange sense of belonging pervades.

Ken continues, "Don't focus on the possibility of failure. Your success is based upon making habits of a few small, successful tasks and repeating them many times, like the beat of hummingbird wings. Eagles don't worry about each wing thrust. You groomed, giving you more confidence; others are attracted to that confidence. You trained to get flight knowledge; your credibility edge grew. As your confidence grew, I believed in you more, but you lacked practice. When you didn't experience immediate success, you gave up. You lost your credibility edge. You became fearful, focusing on your lost confidence, and I also lost confidence in you. That's why I left. You sank like Cephas before his Creator."

The moon brightens the forest. Manfred stands in the center of a moonlit silver patch.

As Ken speaks, Manfred's wings begin moving. He moves them faster until he feels them fill forcefully with air and take on a new shape. He is absorbed in Ken and forgets himself. Unconsciously, Manfred's wings stretched to greater breadth and length. It is automatic and instinctive. He doesn't perceive his rise. Unlike previous attempts, it is automatic and smooth. He rises and looks down. He momentarily loses confidence and starts to roll and flutter.

"Stop focusing on yourself and your failure!" Ken shouts. "Look up!"

Manfred looks up, his flight smoothes and he rises higher. The canopy sinks and the moonlight shines bright on the canopy below. He no longer has the desire to return to the nest. He has a credibility edge sparking a calmness that makes Ken proud. Two eagles join Manfred and they soar in the moonlight. Manfred realizes his talent and gifts. All he needed was the credibility edge.

Dr. John G. Bickert

AH HA MOMENTS

R. Winn Henderson, M.D.

Your significant "Ah Ha" moments in life should not be hard to miss. Yet, when these moments happen, we often fail to notice the little nudges that accompany them. We fail to use the moment's influence in a positive way.

We are surrounded by people who will either encourage or discourage our journey, and it is easy to blame those people for the circumstances in which we find ourselves. However, it is important to understand that we alone are responsible for the "Ah Ha" moments. God uses these moments to get our attention.

Training wheels help us to learn to ride a bicycle. Without them, we would take many tumbles. Life works in much the same way. It would be much easier if we could just learn at an early age to be still and listen to the inner voice with which we are all born. Too often this is not the case. We are born with all the tools we need to live a wonderful life, but sometimes it takes a lifetime to learn how to effectively use these tools to make our lives better, more fulfilling and more joyful.

"Ah Ha" moments are to be treasured. It is in these moments that we change, and it only takes an instant. We cruise through life collecting what we think are the baubles of success and happiness, only to discover that these things will never make us happy. I am no different. I went to medical school and had my share of the toys that money can buy. I had a mansion, a gorgeous wife, and a perfect daughter by my side. Professionally, it felt great to help people who needed my medical attention. I began to devote more and more time to helping my patients. I was on cloud nine and thought that this was happiness.

At the pinnacle of my career as a successful doctor, my world came crashing down. My wife asked for a divorce and moved across the country with my precious daughter. My efforts to make more and more money to keep up our wealthy lifestyle had failed, and the worst possible scenario had played out. This was an "Ah Ha" moment that I failed to recognize. Instead of learning from this lesson, I proceeded to throw myself even deeper into my career, trying to help my patients and employees.

I surrounded myself with needy people in both areas. Even though I was feeding off the power of controlling others, the pressure gauge was spiraling out of control. I hadn't learned the basic principle: the only person you can control is yourself.

Many of my patients looked to me for help with their dependency issues. My new practice had attracted many patients who were searching for a doctor who would simply write them a prescription. I took great pride in not being a pill-pusher and I was determined to get a handle on this area of my practice. I set up a blind study to determine if my patients really needed the medications to which they seemed to be addicted.

This medical study began to return the feedback I needed. My practice had an in-house pharmacy and we generated large amounts of Valium prescriptions. DEA investigators in their "war on drugs" did not recognize that I had a blind study in progress and promptly started an ongoing battle to close me down. My practice began to suffer because the authorities started harassing and intimidating my patients. A year passed and there was no end in sight.

To make a long story short, I disciplined an untrustworthy employee, which led to me becoming the innocent victim in an elaborate entrapment scheme to bribe a public official. I knew that I had not done anything wrong, and two mock trials were conducted that vindicated me. However, at the actual federal trial, I was railroaded into a corner in which evidence that could prove my innocence was not allowed to be presented. To my dismay, the government also threatened my elderly parents if I did not admit to a crime I did not commit.

My "Ah Ha" moment occurred in late November of 2000, when I awoke in jail with questions in my heart. Why had this happened to me? I was innocent, but in prison. I could have easily turned into a cynical, bitter person who blamed someone else for his problems. Instead, I believed there had to be a reason behind what had happened to me.

I knew that I had drifted away from God and His infinite wisdom and guidance, but at this moment of despair, I felt drawn to Him. I opened my heart and asked Him, "Why am I here?" then I lay my head down and went to sleep.

I had a very realistic dream that night that completely changed me in an instant. God spoke to me. All the plans were laid out before me. I now knew what to do with the rest of my life.

I had allowed myself to be attracted to temporary, materialistic things in life and had forgotten to look within myself for the eternal truths. When I awoke, I was filled with a purpose and I had a burning desire to accomplish it. I had the tools I needed and immediately began using them to start the journey that would lead me to the happiness that I had unknowingly been searching for all my life.

My purpose has ultimately been geared to helping others find purpose in their own lives so that they can be happy. Since that "Ah Ha" moment in my cold, dark prison cell, I have never wavered in my determination to do the best that I could to fulfill my mission. Now, with God as my constant companion, I awake each day with a smile on my face and happiness in my heart.

My advice to those reading this book is to recognize the "Ah Ha" moments in your life. Take time to think about the things that are happening in your life. Ask yourself if you are doing the very best that you can to make your life the very best it can be, not only for you but for those around you. Are you using all of the tools you were given at birth to make the world a better place? Do you know your purpose in life?

Look within and listen in silence to the guidance that exists there. You are never alone; God is with you every second of your day. All you have to do is ask and you will receive the answer to all the questions you have ever had. The answers are geared toward bringing out your potential. They will lead you to the peace of mind, contentment, joy and happiness that you so richly deserve.

R. Winn Henderson, M.D.

For more detailed background information, read *Wake Up...Live the Life You Love 1 Best Seller* (page 199) to find out what the dream prophecy was, *Wake Up...Live the Life You Love: A Search For Purpose* (page 134) to find out what the four questions were, and *Wake Up...Live the Life You Love: Giving Gratitude* (page 125) to find out how I got into this situation in the first place.

MY RETURN TO LOVE

Patrick W. O'Connor

There I lay, motionless in bed in a pool of my own blood. "Another failed attempt," I sighed. "Why is this happening to me? I cannot go on!" This is where my story of awakening began.

In the summer of 2000, my life instantly went from darkness to light. I was an MBA graduate with a great job, good looks, beautiful home, sports car, motorcycle, waverunners, girlfriend, friends, family and pretty much everything I thought I ever wanted. On the outside I had it all. There was only one problem: I was suffering from an emptiness so deep I felt as if I was sitting on the edge of a cliff, leaning back on a chair that could be pulled from underneath me at any moment. I found myself in and out of psychiatrists' offices, and on and off depression medications due to several failed suicide attempts. The medications numbed me and the psychiatrists made me feel even more broken.

Every person I talked to said I needed help. "It's like being a diabetic," the doctors said. "You have a chemical imbalance." But through it all, I refused to believe that there was something wrong with me.

Then it happened. One Sunday afternoon I was sitting on my porch when my father called me and asked how I was doing. I said, "You know, Dad, I ought to be doing great. I have everything a guy could want, but something is missing." And in his compassionate, loving, fatherly way he replied, "Maybe you need to return to God." Well, that was a bit of a problem for me, because I was raised Catholic and did not identify with the dogmatic way in which religion was presented to me. But that day, in the midst of my confusion, my father planted a seed of hope. Unknown to me, he had created a doorway to my freedom. I simply had to keep walking.

Two days later I found myself in the parking lot of a Barnes & Noble bookstore. Looking for answers, I went inside and headed for the religion section. I had not been in a bookstore in years, and here I was looking at books I knew I would never read. So I thought, "How about a book on CD?" I reached out and the first audio book I grabbed was *Meditations for Manifesting*, by Dr. Wayne Dyer. I had never heard of Dr. Dyer before, and as far as I knew, the only people who meditated were hippies and New Agers. I sat on the floor for over an hour perusing the other CDs, but Wayne never left my hand. Finally, I decided, "What the heck, I'll buy it."

As I anxiously headed back to my hotel room, I was greeted by an elderly woman in the elevator. She looked down at the CD and said, "Have you ever listened to Wayne Dyer?"

"No," I replied.

"He will change your life forever," she said, with a beautiful, angelic smile. At that moment, a sense of peace filled my body. I thanked her, then proceeded to my dark, empty hotel room. I took off my shoes, sat on the bed and put on my headphones. I had no idea what to expect, but my curiosity was piqued. I gently closed my eyes. From that moment on, I would never see the world the same way again.

Wayne's words filled my ears and penetrated my heart. As I repeated the sounds of "Om" and "Ah," I felt my mind float away. The hour passed effortlessly. As the CD came to an end, I slowly opened my eyes and looked around the room. I saw colors I had never seen before. I heard sounds I had never heard. I felt like a newborn baby entering the world for the first time. It was as if a veil of darkness had been lifted. I walked outside, and to my absolute amazement, everything in life seemed to make sense. I had taken the red pill, left the Matrix, and was downloaded with all of the secrets of the universe. As I was once a drop of water in the ocean, I was now the ocean itself. A huge smile streamed across my face.

This was my awakening. A CD by Wayne Dyer was the seed of love that pierced through my illusion of fear. Everything I had believed up to that point had fallen away in that one hour, as I connected with my truth. From that point on, I was like a sponge. I read and listened to everything I could on Eastern philosophy, religion and meditation. My car had turned into a rolling university; my hotel rooms became sacred spaces to connect with God. People and events began to show up "in color." So-called coincidences and signs were everywhere, directing my every move. When I was with people, I could see and feel their thoughts, feelings and energy. The more I meditated, the clearer I could see my path. I was not sure how or why it happened to me, but I was alive and it felt great.

The more I read, the more I heard about this type of experience happening to others. I suddenly realized why I had resisted all the therapy, drugs and advice to get help during my days of darkness. I was never broken. It was all perfect. I was given exactly what I needed in order to experience the light—to move me closer to God.

We are not broken. It is only the resistance to what *is* that makes us feel this way, but somewhere deep inside we know the truth. We are spiritual beings having a human experience and our purposes here are all the same—to experience the earthly pleasures of life and to evolve into conscious beings of unconditional love and acceptance. Every painful and challenging experience gives us an opportunity to move closer to "mastery." As painful and uncomfortable as they may be, they can be our greatest gifts if we choose to see the divine perfection in them. They enable us to touch others that are struggling as we learn the lessons every master throughout history has taught: unconditional love and acceptance for everyone and everything. This is why we are here.

Gandhi once said, "Be the change you wish to see in the world." *Being* love, *opening* in love and *acting* in love is all it takes. The solution to every problem facing the world today is love. Because, my fellow brothers and sisters… love is who we are and all there is. Everything else, we make up!

Patrick W. O'Connor

I GIVE ALL GLORY TO GOD!

Dr. Heavenly Kimes

I have been a dentist for almost 10 years now. I have owned and operated five dental practices in the Atlanta, Georgia area. Even though I have been very successful, I feel I have another calling in my life.

I have seen many of my colleagues go through careers as physicians and dentists without a financial plan. These doctors have gone though many years of education, committing their lives to helping others. But, despite their benefit to our society, most of them have never taken the time to think of themselves or their future. Despite the glamorous lives of TV doctors, these friends are working in a "rat race." They are paying too much in taxes. Even though they make a lot of money, they do not save for retirement. They don't have time: time to eat properly, to exercise or to share with family.

I am preparing for a crusade to educate professionals—as well as other successful business owners—about how to maximize their tax benefits, and where to put their money so it will work for them. I have spent tens of thousands of dollars on my financial education to learn about stocks, bonds, real estate, insurance and financial services. I have developed proven, predictable and safe techniques to make them millionaires over time. These techniques have worked for me and many others. After all, it is not how much you make, it's how much you keep.

I have been married to my loving husband Dr. Damon Kimes for over 10 years, and I am convinced that success and money mean nothing if you don't have someone to share it with. The definition of success is different for everyone, and to me it means having good health and peace of mind for yourself and your loved ones. As a wealth-building strategist, I teach professionals to set up avenues that allow their money to grow, assuring them they won't have to worry about financial security for their future.

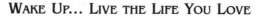

The Lord Jesus Christ is my Savior, and I am living proof that miracles happen. I started my first dental practice with the help of my husband. Within the first year of opening my business, I began to read more than ever and one book in particular sparked my attention: *Rich Dad, Poor Dad*, by Robert Kiyosaki. While reading this book I realized that I only made money if I was physically working; if I did not work, I did not make money. With this in mind, I opened two more practices. I figured if I had offices for other dentists to work in, my income would not be exclusively from my own labor.

As with all of my major decisions, I prayed with my prayer partner from Tennessee prior to the openings. We prayed for the success of the businesses, but also for a sign—I wanted to know this was the plan God had for me.

After the prayer, I scheduled a trip home to Miami to visit my mother for Christmas. I prayed and meditated the whole way, asking God to give me a physical sign that this was what he wanted me to do.

I arrived at my mother's house at about one in the morning. My mother and I sat there and talked until she realized she had forgotten some items needed for the next day's Christmas meal. She asked me to drive her to a 24-hour grocery store. There were hardly any people in the store. I walked around, waiting for my mother to finish her shopping, still praying for a sign to confirm my business venture.

Then a woman approached me and asked me if I was thinking about starting a new business. Surprised, I told her, "Yes." She then told me she was a prophetess and God told her to tell me that I should start my new business. Even though I asked for this confirmation, I was stunned to hear this with my own ears. That day I knew the power of God. And with Him all things are possible. Three years later, I owned five dental practices and was collecting millions of dollars a year. As I embark on a new career to educate others in building wealth, I know God will be there every step of the way.

Dr. Heavenly Kimes

OH, NO! NOT MY SON!

Billie Willmon Jenkin

This shared journey is about my metamorphosis as a woman and parent. I share this so that through my experiences, readers may see their own joy and pain as opportunities for transformation.

I was a woman who had walked a path of guilt, confusing beliefs and anger; one who half heard her wake-up call, but repeatedly hit the "snooze" button. Then I read a letter my older son had written. What he wrote jarred me into consciousness, like smelling smoke in the middle of the night. That jolting wake-up caused me to roll out of bed and hit the floor running: I was clocking in late for fulfilling my purpose.

After marriage, I raised crops, cattle and two sons whom I nurtured with a love of reading and creativity, often inventing stories for their enjoyment. Although we attended church, I didn't instill values for accepting people who were "different." I specifically taught my sons to view homosexuals negatively. Little did I realize that my prejudice would nearly lead to the death of my elder son.

After both sons entered college, I re-evaluated my life, desiring to re-create it with meaning and joy. Freshly divorced—like an eager puppy darting through an open gate—I raced from marital restraint to blind spontaneity. My first few months of merrymaking hit a speed bump when I heard the words no parent wants to hear, *"Mom, I'm gay."*

My grief was comparable to having learned my son was dead: numbness, disbelief, heartache, guilt, shame, blame. "What have I done wrong? Why did he choose this? *Where is God?*" Regardless of my confusion, I knew Rusty needed assurance of my love more than ever. When we finally spoke face-to-face, tears of joy and relief flowed unashamedly down Rusty's cheeks: I knew I had conveyed unconditional love and acceptance.

Knowing I loved to dance and was willing to attend a favorite nightspot with him, Rusty invited me to a mostly-gay club. A young man noticed my resemblance to Rusty and approached me to confirm, "You're Rusty's mom, aren't you?" When I nodded and smiled, his eyes moistened and filled.

Clasping my hand, he confided, "I would give *anything* if my mother would come here with me...if she'd just *speak* to me." The young man continued, as if a dam had burst. "My dad's a preacher. When they learned I was gay, they threw me out and haven't spoken to me since. They thought if the congregation knew about me, Dad wouldn't be respected."

While Rusty and I celebrated our new relationship, the young man stared forlornly at us. Although my heart could hear his cry, I ignored that call.

Later, Rusty explained his own experiences growing up: Although popular in school with faculty and peers, he had lived in terror of his "awful problem." He had believed his feelings (even though he wasn't acting on them) had condemned him to eternal damnation. Unable to overcome his emotions, he had spent his teen years begging God to make him "normal." Rusty calmly admitted that with his prayers unanswered, he had considered suicide. With his serene attitude—and because these thoughts had occurred years earlier—I felt tranquil.

Satisfied with my relationships and generally pleased with my life, my journey of change brought me to a point where I defined my purpose—something familiar, but never recognized. My purpose in life is to empower others to appreciate the significance of their lives and to find peace in the midst of "what is."

How I would apply my purpose to the benefit of others remained a mystery. But soon, Rusty shared with me a letter he had written to the troubled mother of another gay man: "The worst insult...is to call someone a fag.... We end up believing we are the lowest life form on the planet. Self-esteem is virtually non-existent. We put on a mask and hope that no one can see behind it and find out what we really are—all because of these feelings we did not choose. I battled with those feelings for years and years, contemplated suicide several times, twice had knives to my wrists, and once had a loaded shotgun in my mouth…."

Brrinnnggg! The wake-up call! No soft whisper I could stifle this time, nor did I wish to. For the first time, I realized the extent of my son's torment, how close I had come to losing him, and how I had augmented his shame and anguish. I wondered how many gay and lesbian teens *had* followed through with their suicide plans, and how many bereaved parents remained wondering, "*Why?*"

Immediately, I yearned to use my experience, compassion and skills to support young gays, lesbians and their parents in the turbulent process of "coming out." What could I do to support *all* young people, whose emotional security—or insecurity—is established long before sexual orientation is known?

At the time I learned of Rusty's near-suicide, I was writing and illustrating a children's book developed from a story I had made up for my young sons. Uncomfortably, I realized I had created a magical, "feel-good" ending to the tale, not a conscious, purposeful story to support children in their struggle for self-acceptance. I wanted to change the story to enhance self-esteem in all children, regardless of their sexual orientation, academic prowess, good looks or popularity.

Top preschools have two- and three-year waiting lists, demonstrating parental dedication to excellence in offspring. Proud are the parents whose children are honor students, whose sons excel in football, whose daughters are beautiful or whose children other parents envy for whatever reason. Do the "average" children all vanish into oblivion? Does society simply ignore them?

Like Humpty-Dumpty, a child's shattered self-image seems impossible to restore. Taking heed of my son's despair, my wake-up call urged me to support children's eggshell-fragile spirits. After re-evaluating my objectives, I revisited my purpose and rewrote my book. Now *The Knock-Kneed Cowboy* has a hero who learns to celebrate his uniqueness instead of mimicking others.

As my first children's book nears its release date, I am not dreaming of a Newbury or Caldecott Medal (typically considered the highest American honors for children's literature). Rather, I am excited about the intangible reward of empowering others—especially children—to appreciate their own value and to find peace within.

My journey is still an exciting, winding road. Today I know that had I not had the now-cherished gift of a child who is "different," I would never have re-created my life and enjoyed the acceptance of self and others, peace with my Maker and mankind, and the meaning and joy that life now holds. Nor would I be motivated in the same way to touch the lives of those who are hurting, whose pain I have experienced.

Just as people's strengths, purposes and beliefs vary greatly, so do our wake-up calls differ. Your journey—like mine—will depend on your unique characteristics and the people and circumstances along your path. In our journeys, may we each grow in appreciation of ourselves, our fellow travelers and the diversity which makes us who we are.

Billie Willmon Jenkin

WHOSE LIFE ARE YOU REALLY LIVING?

Simon Graham

So, you've been to all the self-help seminars, guru workshops and high-energy motivational speakers. You've even read the books in a never-ending quest to find your inner passion—that special purpose that stokes and fuels the fires for your life—but passion still eludes you. Does that sound familiar?

I share this personal story with you in hope that you may identify with me, and as a result, learn to break down your perceived barriers so that you can move forward on the quest to find your life's purpose. Mark Twain once said, "I can show anybody how to get what they want out of life. The problem is I can't find anyone who knows what they want!"

Why is it so hard to find our purpose in life? After all, stories abound about people living their passions and finding their purpose. For some, it's raising children. For others, it is building a successful business, writing an epic movie or preparing a delectable meal for connoisseurs. But for many, this magical discovery continues to elude them.

Many in today's society are well-versed in the concepts of body, mind and spirit. The beginning stages of our lives are consumed so with the "body," that the matters of mind and spirit usually don't come up until later.

As a child in Tasmania, Australia, I was an uninhibited little boy who embraced his surroundings with awe and wonder, not yet aware of reality's rules. My spirit was full of joy and serenity. Somehow, along the way, the essence of that childhood freedom slowly faded as I began to learn and experience—sometimes painfully—the rules of the body.

During these formative years, the laws of the body took priority over mind and spirit. They were all about survival—survival of the fittest. Without the knowledge or ability to make the body survive, the spirit cannot project itself.

My mum and dad lovingly played their parental roles close to perfection, protecting, guiding and teaching me the rules for survival—education, nutrition, finance, career, exercise, communication, etc. I didn't know it at the time, but my "survival" knowledge slowly assimilated some of my parents' traits, ideals, behaviors and belief systems. Some of them over-rode my own innate traits, thus suppressing and partially obscuring my real self. This is, by no means, a negative comment about my parents. They provided the foundation for me to live the life I love to the fullest. But as I grew older and advanced closer to the responsibilities of adulthood, I noticed an increasing lack of confidence in some aspects of my life—an emptiness totally devoid of passion.

I considered my upbringing to be nearly perfect. I'd ask myself, "How can I possibly be unhappy? I've heard plenty of people who've risen from 'not-so-perfect family life' to lead very successful lives, but here I am, having lived a charmed childhood, but unhappy!" Each day was a struggle to understand the persistent roller coaster of my extreme emotional peaks and troughs. Logic would say there was something seriously wrong with me. It was this thought that chipped away at my foundation of confidence. Time did the rest. Luckily, my inner spirit never caved in. Upon reflection, it gently guided me along that long and winding path to success.

Although it wasn't apparent at the time, my parents' insistence that I study at the strict Christian Brothers College was a blessing in disguise. That was a defining period I often reflect upon—for two years I studied other people's beliefs. During that time, I was exposed to religions other than my own Catholicism—Buddhism, Hinduism, Shintoism, Judaism and Islam. This opened my mind to the world and gave me the deeper understanding required to see my fellow man as one and the same.

In the midst of this religious adventure, I happened upon the benefits of meditation and quiet self-reflection. Returning to those disciplines, I realized that part of my self—my true, real, full self—was obscured under some of my father's strong traits, traits that were his gifts, not mine. I was still living some of the ideals I had assimilated from his well-meaning guidance. It's difficult to find your course and live your passion if somebody else's traits are overriding your own unique gifts. It tempers your ability to feel the pure emotion required to truly experience passion.

Are you having trouble finding your passion or purpose in life? If so, then ask yourself, "Am I unconsciously living someone else's ideals while suppressing my own?" Listen to your gut feeling—your intuition—it knows the answer. You simply need to take the time to listen to yourself and be patient. Each individual has his own unique gifts. You must let these gifts rise up from underneath the protective layer of your persona.

I've always had a love for learning new things. My philosophy had been to share my time mastering many things rather than devoting my entire life to being the best at just one thing. To me, learning about new things meant living the life I loved; however, little did I know I was only experiencing a small fraction of the joy of learning. Not until the day I started to use my knowledge to teach and share with others did my passion for life explode through the roof. My main source of happiness is no longer centered on accumulating riches. Rather, it comes from the humble act of making a difference in someone's life by teaching them something new.

This has only been a recent discovery in my life, so my journey has only just begun. With each step, my confidence increases. As long as I keep walking, I trust the universe to make it an exciting journey. I feel my story is different. It's not one of troubled beginnings or adverse environments as often seen in self-help books and success stories. It's a simple story that proves we all have problems during our lives and that we're perfectly normal, but it's not okay to ignore the problem without also seeking its source. Just as you progress in school, the master plan of life progresses to a new adventure that expands your existence. You should never stop learning. The moment learning stops, you decline. Change is constant. Your

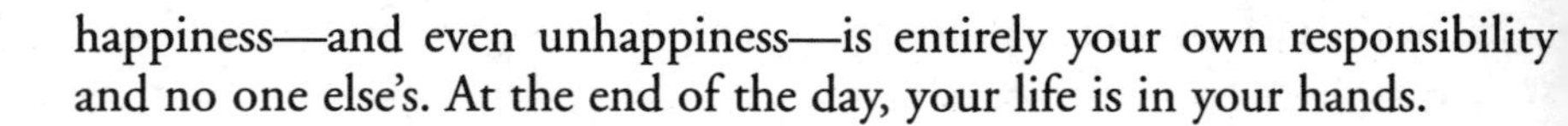

happiness—and even unhappiness—is entirely your own responsibility and no one else's. At the end of the day, your life is in your hands.

Simon Graham

YOUR BLISSFUL LIFE

Timothy A. McGinty

Deep within all of us lies the desire for ultimate happiness in every part of our lives. For years it seemed as though true happiness was out of my reach. Despite all I had achieved, something was still missing: Something was not right. Why wasn't I happy? The more I focused and the harder I tried to grasp it, the farther it seemed to move away from me.

Does this sound familiar? If it describes the place you are in right now, you know it is a frustrating place. I know, I've been there. I call this feeling "the struggle." The challenge is that you don't know how to move past it. Until now. Before you can "Live the Life You Love," you must define what that life is to you. I call it "Your Blissful Life."

How do you discover "Your Blissful Life?" There is a systematic approach. This process enabled me to discover my blissful life and it changed me forever. It was so empowering, so freeing, so exhilarating that I must share it with everyone.

Everyone at some point experiences "the struggle." Regardless of age, race, gender, religion or socio-economic status, we have all experienced the struggle in some area of our lives. However, this struggle is rocking us to the core of who we are. It is rocking us to the core because it is a conflict between various aspects of ourselves. These aspects are often referred to as "parts" or "components" of our lives.

You must unconditionally accept the struggle you are experiencing. Embrace your struggle with all your heart and soul. It is a part of you and it makes you a unique individual. Millions of people around the world are currently experiencing, or will experience, similar thoughts and feelings. Once you finally decide to recognize it and accept the fact that you are in the midst of "the struggle," you can begin to move past it. My recognition and acceptance of "the struggle" gave me the freedom and permission to do so. What does your recognition and acceptance give you?

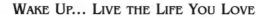

Your recognition and acceptance enables you to start defining "Your Blissful Life." The following process enables you to start on your journey of discovery. Name all of the parts of your life. Most people immediately identify the more common parts such as father, brother, sister, mother, significant other, career, golfer, bowler, friends, or musician just to name a few. We are all made up of many parts. Simply list them as you identify them. Is there any part that is truly important to you that you have pushed aside?

Which parts are involved in the struggle? It is important to identify these by placing an asterisk next to the name; these are the parts you will want to work with first. Rank your parts in order of importance to you. This provides you with a clear understanding of what is most important to you. Which part of your life is most important?

Specifically define what you want in each part that you have identified. When I reached this step of the process, I asked myself the question, "What is my ultimate goal for this part?" I then answered it in detail. I described how I would feel once I achieved it, what I and others would be saying about me, and finally, all of the changes I would see. This enables you to clearly define what you want and how you will know when you have achieved it.

You then move on to defining what impact this will have on your life. Note how your life changes when you get exactly what you want. Ask yourself if you are willing to do what it takes to achieve your ultimate goal, no matter what it may be. How badly do you want this for yourself? Finally, how will getting what you want for this part fit in with your other parts? Are there any conflicts? If so, review the parts in conflict until you are satisfied with both goals. I found that there were actually very few conflicts, because when I sat down and focused on what I truly wanted, all of my parts seemed to naturally align themselves.

Congratulations! You have just started your journey towards defining "Your Blissful Life!" Notice how good you feel at this moment. Multiply this feeling by one million. This is how you will feel when you complete the process for every part. You can now continue walking toward "Your Blissful Life." You must execute a Personal Contract with yourself: a simple, written statement that affirms that you are ready, willing and able to do whatever it takes to get exactly what you want for this part. Stating your goals is dreaming; writing them down and committing to them by using your Personal Contract is called goal setting.

Now that you have committed to your goals, you need to develop your course of action for achieving them. How do you plan to get from your current location to "Your Blissful Life?" This course will lead you to your promised land. Once you define your path, you will automatically move toward it, because the only destination possible is "Your Blissful Life". So how do you develop your plan?

You develop your plan by selecting one of your parts and re-reading your goal for it. Now, close your eyes and imagine you have already achieved your goal. Really get into that moment. Hear yourself, see yourself, and notice how good it feels having achieved your goal. Now, as you stand in your moment, look back to now and describe all the actions you took to get to this moment, right here, right now. These actions become your action plan for this part. Repeat this process for every one of your parts.

The final step in the process is action. You must take action in order to achieve "Your Blissful Life" and live the life you love. If you have had issues with taking action in the past, you will find that it is now easy because you know exactly where you are headed. You are headed toward the destination you desire most, "Your Blissful Life!"

It has now been three years since I utilized this process. Today my life is filled with so much freedom, happiness and joy that I pinch myself daily. It feels as though I am floating with the clouds. The life that I once thought was unreachable is now alive and well within me. It is within you, too. What is "Your Blissful Life?"

Timothy A. McGinty

WRITING LIFTS ME UP

Ena M. Simms

I gasp for air, not knowing if I will get enough,
A glorious feeling just for one more day.
My mind wanders and then I stare.
Why am I really here?
I run here, run there not much doing, yet thinking,
"Success is not very hard to get,
But it is definitely not like making a bet,
Because without that glimmer of hope, you will never be set."

My earlier life has been focused, though not attaining much,
But even as a young child with limited opportunities, I prayed to be the best,
Since living in the West Indies could really put your talent to the test.
My avid determination of going to high school was achieved,
But this was done because I held tight to my beliefs,
Since my lack of money to pay for the school fees might have led me straight to the streets.

Many days I awaken with murmuring anxiety,
Today I will achieve, today I will achieve,
But what, what will it be?

My math skills, reading skills, geography and even cooking skills
But writing, I crave because with new ideas
I was becoming very brave.
I would write about little feelings, ill wills and,
Oh, sometimes the venting ideas commanded time to stand still.

Real life, with its echoes of bellows and blows
Have whipped me right and sometimes way below.
With a lonely feeling of being discarded,
I search my soul, just to really know, what it is that I wanted.

What place is there that I still don't know?
What should I do, where should I go?
Get ready to behold and embrace.
Go embark and finally capture some of the unknown.

In the burrows of anxiety, I dig myself out.
Get up, get out, move on to take a stand.
Waive to the world, I am coming, yes I am coming,
With success blazing in my soul.

The writing is on the wall,
I will no longer fall.
I take each step with ease, and sometimes wonder,
"Who is there for me to please?"
A life full of silent moments, unspoken dreams
Sometimes unrealistic expectations, but nevertheless
A quenching desire to be the best?

By using reading as a soother, a comfort food for my soul
I acquired hundreds of books, Oh yes, I prefer this to be untold.
My books became a total cushion for my mind to behold.
Good books, great books, mediocre books,
You name it, I was sold.
Yet, the crave—the hollow—was still there for me to endure.

As I go about my daily chores, sometimes singing,
Sometimes laughing, working with mind ablaze,
Clearing my thoughts of muddled woes,
The anxious spring of words would pop up in my mind.
A few words, a sentence, a paragraph
Many times leading into an entire collage of beautiful thoughts.
But being a singer was definitely not where I belong.

The exchange of words, suddenly became like magic.
Do not waste them. Never let them disappear.

Embrace them, use them, let them help you to have your say.
Since each word is an opening, pointing me to the right way.
I just cannot wait for that special day.

In moments of deep concentration, a subtle idea becomes a deep accomplishment.
"Go and write it down. Go now, and write it down,"
The gentle voice within whispers,
With hasty steps and a muddled mind,
I grabbed a sheet of paper.

Just let the words flow, the thoughts unfold,
Why worry? Just empty your soul.
To my surprise, the page was full,
And as I said before, it feels like time stands still.
With squinting eyes and galloping thoughts,
I try to review the contents that were brought
To the forefront of my mind;
Alas it's done, it's done.

This is a song, brought on by the sun, in a burning beam in my heart.
It is definitely not just any thought.
Though some tough times pushed me against a wall,
I was determined that the lack of trying
Was never going to be my downfall.
The writing I enjoy was never taken to a very high level earlier in my life.

However, I experienced an immediate change when I was forced to deal with an anxious moment. A few years ago I was taking some courses at a university while I worked full-time and was raising three children on my own. Each student was required to prepare a 15-page essay on a selection of topics. I did what I thought was correct and was grateful that it was completed.

Alas, the test papers were marked and handed back to the class. Everyone expressed joy or sorrow according to the grades they received. For me, there was no grade. I did the wrong question. In a total moment of humiliation, I could not share the anguish I felt.

The teacher gracefully called me aside and offered me time to redo the paper. Though I was thankful for her thoughtfulness, I still felt stupid, alone and lost. My comfort level did not allow me to share my feelings with anyone in the class. After the class, my journey home by train and bus was a long one, so I had time to reflect. What happened next was a very natural thing for me. I started to write–to bring out my:

Delayed Feelings

What happened in the last little while? I wonder and stare.
As my eyes were drawn to the Holy Book, beware, beware.
Tears bubble up inside, as I dare not to cry,
But uncontrollably, they come dripping slowly from my eyes.

Tears of joy, tears of sorrow, a mixture, what? It's not about tomorrow
The silence has been broken, the pain I will no longer borrow.
For now, it is what is felt and the deep overcomes the hollow.

At last, at last, my arms are ready to embrace
With the unrest of my heart taking its proper place,
A place to reach out, a place to accept
With hands stretched out to humanity,
No longer ready for any rejects.

The past, though not totally forgotten, is left behind.
The present, I will take one day at a time,
As I move forward in God's care,
I pledge not to harbor any fears,

But move in total dignity with a tremendous value for integrity,

I will continue as God guides and clears the path of my life
And gives me a chance to move forward one step at a time.

Writing, to me, is like enjoying a sauna: a whirlpool of great thoughts. Whenever I am awake, or even in my dreams, from the moment I realized that writing was a pathway to cleanse my soul, I never looked back or worried. As I breathe I write, as I write I also breathe.

Ena M. Simms

LIVING THE ADVENTURE OF LIFE

Phil Conway

How many of us actually take the time to practice gratitude in our daily lives? Can you really afford to continue to wait for the right moment? You would need inspiration from your inner soul to live the best life you can, enjoying the abundance of life, great health, great relationships and great spirituality while contributing to society. What would it take to motivate you to take action right now?

Along with my brother, Kevin, I am proud to be part of the family's fourth generation funeral service. We work with my father, Frank, and Ben and Maureen Brodeur. Our firm is privileged to have a wonderful, dedicated and loyal staff consisting of more than 20 full- and part-time assistants who help us carry out our mission to partner with families and help them commemorate the lives of their own special heroes. It is my hope that you would use your imagination to create whatever dream you desire and then be able to achieve your goals so you may live the best life possible.

This "thing" called death can be discussed on many levels. I use it to motivate since one never truly knows when death may happen. At the very core of our being, we are just personalities. Some take the position that they are spiritual but not religious. Some people participate in faith-based communities. Others may deny the existence of any higher power. This is where I find beauty in the human species. It allows for individual will and the ability to decide what is best for each of us. Our personalities are the expressions of the spirit within. I am grateful for my personal and spiritual relationship with God and my roots within the Roman Catholic faith.

As I work with families, I get the chance to help them remember the person who died. "Died." It's a four letter word but, then again, so is "life." When these two words are juxtaposed, an interesting paradox emerges.

We gather at times of death for someone's funeral. Though a painful time, we are also celebrating the life of the deceased. In the words of an expression I borrow from fellow colleagues and use often, "We gather not because someone died, but because they lived."

Much is written about consoling those who experience loss. We all have various views regarding death, including what role that person played in the lives of the living family and the kind of social connections they enjoyed. Helping a family tell the story of John Doe's life with a series of planned events brings so many rewards—most often grateful hugs and kisses for helping to coordinate the details of the person's story.

In my career, I have the privilege of offering compassionate care for the living and respectful custodial care for the deceased. Those who practice funeral services share in listening to stories about the dead as told by the living. The next step is planning an event that succinctly tells the story, provides meaning to the family and friends, validates the family's sense of loss, and recreates the person's story.

Wouldn't you agree we all have a story? Some may be more colorful than others; some are simple. I would say, "If you don't have a story, you aren't living life!" You will experience losses of all kinds in life. For example, I've lost keys, important papers or a sports game. In sports, we learn there is no experience like winning—especially with dignity, grace, honor and respect. I ask you to keep in mind that losing also has its challenges—especially for competitive people—yet, there is nothing quite like that experience either. I was always told that it shapes your character. As life progresses, we deal with the issues at hand and then move on. Let's start a new mind-set as you substitute the word change for loss.

Many people have a difficult time dealing with change. Many resources exist to help develop the necessary skills to embrace change in our lives. I understand our brain wants to keep the status quo. So, it acts on the law of inertia: a body at rest tends to stay at rest. That struggle against change leads to emotional turmoil, and we can sense all the stress and pain of loss. The intensity varies, and there are paths that will bring us to joy; just in a different way than before the loss. Death is not optional. Being a companion to the bereaved allows for social support, validation, and listening in order to help others deal with the loss and change. The holistically healthy mind-set will evolve into building its new identity in life.

When you read this, remember one important point: This story is not about me, it's about how to reach the special person in you. You have an inner genius, just champing at the bit to move your ideas forward. Time is one resource that cannot be paused. It may take a leap of faith—even writing down some of the obstacles in your life. How can you realize that they may serve in helping you be grateful for lessons learned if you aren't sure what they are? Are they blessings in disguise? Or are they merely a test to determine your clarity and intensity of desire?

My hope is that you are able to achieve a state of humility in order to be grateful for people, things, and events in your life. Let's use this to understand we all can achieve our goals, and it does not require sacrifice and struggle. Life is easy. Money comes easy. Friendships come easy. Love comes easy. Contributions to society, family and strangers come easy. Is world peace that far away? Let's appreciate each other, and live in the manner that God wants us to live—to love Him and our neighbor. What wonderful life lies ahead for you?

Phil Conway

TREASURE MAP

Conrad Raw

What if you had a clear road map that would lead you to living the life you love? Would you use it, or would you prefer to pull in to a rest stop and watch everyone else drive by? Would you take action and live your dreams, or would you fall asleep at the wheel as life passes you by?

In your hands you are holding a book full of inspiration from people who have experienced life as you could be doing—testimonials from real people who can tell you it is possible to live life on your own terms.

I wish I had had this book when I began. I find great joy in sharing my story with you, and hope it will inspire you, reassure you and much more. My hope is that my story will fuel you to take action. So even though this story is about me, it is also about you.

My journey started with a daydream. When I was in school, teachers often scolded me for daydreaming during their classes, but I simply found the stories that were evolving in my mind more interesting than the things they were trying to force into me. Yet, whenever I had to write a story for school, I ended up getting a bad grade. One day, however, something strange happened. There was a national contest for teenagers to write a short story that would be judged by published authors. Although my entire class participated, I was the only student to win a prize. My teachers told my parents, "Conrad is already living a different story."

As a teenager, I had a picture in my mind of the type of life I wanted. Maybe it wasn't clear in the beginning, but it was a start. I found joy in discovering what the human mind is capable of beyond the limited beliefs and restrictions placed on us by society. I wanted to earn plenty of money while still having enough time to travel the globe. I wanted to learn first-hand what was really possible with the extremely powerful instrument we all have—the mind. I wouldn't dare put a limit on the potential we each have, but most people have no idea what they can achieve.

I ended up with a degree in law. This still amazes me, but my aunt, who practices fortune-telling, told me at the beginning of my studies that I would not become a lawyer—she said I would teach. I thought she was wrong. I simply couldn't imagine myself as a teacher—I was actually afraid to speak in front of an audience.

I had to work very hard before and during exams so I could use the rest of my time to study the human mind and the abilities that remain dormant in most people. I wrote the main outline for my book during this time and I finished law school with honors. Now, some years later, I have given international seminars and speeches; I am actually making a living by teaching others to activate their higher human potential.

I am now living the life I love and would like to share with you what I learned so that you might be inspired to do the same.

The quality of your life is directly linked to the questions you ask yourself. I created my life on my own terms by asking myself, "What do I want my life to be?" I thought this was a normal question to ask, but through my seminars I have discovered that most people do not ask this question. Instead they let others dictate how their lives should be lived. Most people choose—whether consciously or unconsciously—the "safest" way; the way many others took before them. Many end up living unfulfilled lives because of this.

I strongly believe the key to living a fulfilling life is spending as much time as possible on your passions—the things that give you great joy. This is the path on which you can find your life's purpose. We get energizing joy as a result because it is what we are meant to do. It is then that we function in a way that is truly in tune with our core—our soul.

The other important question to ask yourself is, "How?" You may also ask, "If it were possible to do this, how would I?" It is like climbing a poorly lit staircase—you know you want to get to the next floor, but you can't see each individual step. You just have to climb it step-by-step. You can't see the next step until you've stepped on the previous one. Each step can be climbed by asking the "how" question. Although you will find obstacles and challenges on your way, take them as an opportunity to learn and grow. This is how you climb those steps. If you live according to your purpose, things become easier along the way. Once you reach the top, you might even discover there is another floor.

Another key aspect of the fulfilling life is providing value to others. If you live your life in a way that benefits others, many opportunities will open up for you. If you want to earn tons of money, find out how you can provide as much value to others as possible while doing so. It is your responsibility to reach beyond a mediocre life. If you don't, you will not only be short-changing yourself, but many others who could have grown from your contribution as well.

What will you do? Will you keep doing what you've always done or start living the life you love? What is the first step you can take to change your life for the better? Start today: Draw the map, check your compass, and go find the treasure, living the life you love.

Conrad Raw

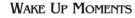

OH, OLIVER! (FROM THE WAKE UP LIVE MOVIE)

Liz Vassey

I was a very, very, very shy kid, when I was three or four. I just didn't talk to strangers and I was very uncomfortable in front of groups.

I started acting when I was nine, and I started in theater—actually musical theater. It was then that I saw my sister in a play, and I went to my mom, and I said, "I think I would really like to try that." She said, "Oh, I think that would be great. I'm not taking you. Your sister can take you out. I don't want any part of seeing you get up on that stage and seeing what happens."

The first play I auditioned for was *Oliver* and I sang for it, and I played Oliver. I remember getting up on that stage and actually feeling very much at home for the first time.

Once you've had that moment, I would say you have to be incredibly persistent. Do not believe too much of the good or of the bad. Stay true to yourself because they are trying to change you and fix you and mold you. I think what's different or peculiar about you is what's special about you in the first place. Don't lose it.

Liz Vassey

SEEK, ASK, KNOCK AND RECEIVE

Jan Holdmann

If you are actually awake and living the life you love, you are reveling in every new "aha" moment. But, how do you get to that point? Most people never do. It's not because they don't want to, but rather because they get stuck and don't know how to go on. The good news is that there are answers available to every one of us. I found one while swinging from the end of my proverbial rope.

I have spent a lot of time working on myself mentally, emotionally and spiritually. I have tried to live a life of Christian love as I understand it. I actually worked very hard at staying "up" and "positive," looking for the best in every situation and for God in each face I met; I aimed to be grateful for my experiences and look for the lessons, if not the joys, of trying to do "God's will."

It appeared I was living an enviable life—at least that is what I was told by friends. That is definitely not how I felt. I felt lonely and sad, as if putting onc foot in front of the other was just one step too many. I thought, "If this is how this game is supposed to be played, I don't want to play any more." It felt that doing the right thing better reap some rewards in Heaven because it sure didn't do much for me on Earth. I was sick and tired of just getting by, always taking one step forward and two steps back.

I discovered one morning that my second marriage of 22 years was over. I was in my mid-fifties and a two-time failure. My sister needed a second kidney transplant after her body had rejected the first one. After months of waiting, I was finally cleared to be a donor, but the whole process and aftermath were still frightening for her and the rest of the family.

I decided to start fresh and moved from the Midwest to the Phoenix area. I bought a house large enough to help my sister and brother-in-law make a new beginning. My 87-year-old mother, who had Parkinson's Disease, would spend her winters with me and her summers in Michigan for as long as possible. That first fall, I got a job selling health insurance. However, before I could even write a policy for myself, I shattered my knee cap. When they operated on my knee, they removed some of the hardware in my ankle from a prior injury. Complications arose, and I was informed I would have to wear a metal brace on my ankle for the rest of my life—my driving ankle no less. I was grateful for the brace at the time because it allowed me to walk, but I vowed I would not wear it one minute longer than necessary.

I still couldn't sell insurance. In Phoenix, nearly anywhere you schedule an appointment will be at least an hour away. The pain from my knee and ankle was so intense from driving, I couldn't sleep at night, then I couldn't function the following day. Even though I had been a senior manager in a mid-sized company for 14 years and had been recorded in the 1996 International *Who's Who of Professional Management Directory*, I couldn't find a job interview in corporate America. I had worked with seniors in Illinois, providing long-term care, Medicare supplements, life insurance and annuities. I was a past member of Toastmasters International, a motivational speaker, a workshop leader and author, and I was completely dumbfounded. I had no constructive words left.

I let loose with a bitterness I had never allowed to surface before. I didn't curse God, but I cursed everything else. I believe we are responsible and accountable for our lives and we draw to us that which we put out there. If that is a law, and I am convinced it is, what about all my efforts to "live right," to love myself, others and God and to do the right thing? I cried, "I give up! This time I really mean it. I surrender." I railed on about trying, doing and being, and it never working out. "What? Am I not good enough for you, God? I can't and won't live this way, anymore! Take me. Take me now. Either take me home or use me, but I am not doing this anymore. You do what you need to, but I am done!"

I scared my family. They had rarely seen me outside the role I played of big sister, caretaker and encourager. I was the strong one who could handle anything and find the silver lining. Do you think that might be why

the universe kept throwing anything and everything in my path? Of course it was.

My life started to turn right side up. I met people with information who helped me move forward. I received checks in the mail I didn't even know were owed to me. Out of the blue, I was offered a job selling life insurance and annuities for a respectable company, and I could even do it part-time. The job was exactly what I asked for. It was something I could enjoy. I could be proud of the product and help I provided, earn enough money to get out of debt and even allow myself time to pursue my work, to live the life I love and to help others do the same. After redesigning my own physical therapy, I no longer wear that metal brace on my ankle. I've even managed to wear high heels occasionally.

You see, the worst year of my life produced the keys to give me a better future. It gave me that "aha" moment when I surrendered with intention and expectation and changed my life completely. It has prompted me to start writing my new book, *Seek, Ask, Knock and Receive.*

Here is the short version of the formula:

Seek–Be aware. Recognize the dissatisfaction.
Ask–Ask with intention for the answers and guidance you want.
Knock–On God's door, as though you expect it to be opened.
Receive–Be prepared. Expect and be willing to receive. Do it with gratitude.

It's the formula for my "break-through break-down" and for how I am living in my life now. I consciously use this formula in my work, for my family and for my physical and spiritual well-being. I am free and, more importantly, I am happy to be me.

Jan Holdmann

HEAL YOURSELF: LIFE DEPENDS ON IT

Susie Beiler

I have been doing it consciously for the past three years. I will continue to do it as long as I walk this earth. As I heal myself on deeper and deeper levels, the mysteries of my soul unravel and purpose is revealed.

In the year 2000, I was diagnosed with Chronic Fatigue Syndrome. As I heal the core issues of spiritual and emotional oppression that caused this problem, I empower myself to be free from the blocks and entanglements that hold me back from my life's purpose. I have discovered that I can choose healing through joy or struggle. Throughout my conscious journey, I have received support as I opened my heart to others. I have been given the knowledge that I can navigate my own way as I journey through life. We are all given this gift. I am grateful that I choose to unwrap it each and every day. I am learning to listen to the beat of my own heart and follow where it leads. I am discovering the amazing gift of living as a powerful person and the blessings that I can give to others as I accept my life purpose.

The power and the interconnections between my spiritual awareness, emotions, thoughts and physical being continue to astound me. I am capable of letting go of illness as I look within and discover the underlying pattern that "caused" it. For example, I recently started to develop a sinus infection. As I looked at my current situation and reflected upon my life, I noticed a pattern revealing that whenever I got sinus infections in the past, it was because I craved attention and nurturing but did not know how to speak up and ask for it. At the time I got sick, I was giving attention and nurturing to everything and everyone else but myself. Once it was clear that I needed to nurture myself and I didn't need a sinus infection to remind me to do this, the illness "miraculously" vanished within a period of a few minutes. Every physical, mental or emotional ailment is a clue to something we need to heal on a deeper level within ourselves. The physical body is a place where the need for healing shows up because we do not pay attention to ourselves until we are sick. This includes cancer, broken bones, diabetes, heart disease—the list goes on. The diagnosis is irrelevant. The message from the diagnosis is to look within for healing. There is a place for doctors, chiropractors, psychologists and every professional in the healing field. Ultimately, however, you are your own healer. You know what is best for your body. While it may serve its purpose, a medication can never tell you what you *really* need. This is only a bandage. True healing comes from within. It comes from you, not something or someone outside of yourself.

Every day you create health or disease depending on your choices. We can all heal ourselves. Consider the example of a paper cut. When you get a paper cut and you just let it heal without any creams or medications, it heals on its own. Your body's immune system is equipped to heal that cut. Each of us has an immune system. Our job is to dislodge the interferences that prevent it from doing its work. For some, that may be as simple as drinking more water. For most of us, however, healing ourselves involves some form of deep spiritual and emotional work to let go of old ways of being. As you let go of oppression or fear or whatever your obstacle may be and simply allow yourself to fully accept each experience as it comes, your physical body will transform itself before your own eyes. Ultimately, it is the beliefs you hold in your mind and heart about your own ability to heal that govern your results.

Healing yourself requires you to dig deep in *all* areas of your life. It is an amazing process that requires commitment, support and courage. Your food, your emotions, your thoughts and your connection to the Divine are all pieces of the puzzle that is you.

You must address your stress and face yourself. You experience stress when you are functioning in ways that do not support your true purpose. Stress is simply a separation from your essence. What is your purpose on this earth? Can you carry it out in your current condition or do you first need to see yourself as the light that you truly are? Be grateful for being a healed person. See yourself as healed and give yourself permission to experience joy in your daily life. Go out into nature and be physically active. Spend

time with encouraging friends. Do the things you enjoy and feed your soul. Cultivate a good relationship with yourself. You have to live the rest of your life with you.

This is not a solitary process. Although you are the only person who can heal your own life, you need guidance and support. Remember that whatever you are experiencing, you are never alone. Even when it seems you are going through it by yourself, spirit is always there to encourage and strengthen you. Ask for support and guidance, and be ready and willing to accept it, even if it comes in an unexpected way. If you open your heart to receiving, friends and family are usually there to cheerlead or at least lend listening ears. Believe that the people in your life who truly love you want to see you happy; they want the best for you. Your happiness is your decision, but gather a support troupe for the times when it seems more difficult to choose joy.

This is a call to do what you came here to do. You came to this Earth to heal yourself. In so doing, the vibration of the planet is raised and the Earth heals as well. The ripples of your healing extend to the farthest reaches of the universe. It is imperative that you buckle down and get to work—and have some fun, too. Your life depends upon it. All life everywhere depends upon it.

Susie Beiler

FALLING FORWARD

Chuck Carstensen

In the book *Think and Grow Rich*, author Napoleon Hill said the 500 most successful men he had known told him that "Their greatest success came just one step beyond the point at which defeat had overtaken them."

I get excited when I think about that. That really motivates me. Let me tell you why. Defeat and failure have paid me a visit more than once, but all the times defeat had visited me, it was before I read this quotation. So on all previous occasions I did what everyone else does: I quit. The average person doesn't want the embarrassment of failure and defeat, so they run from it by quitting and coming up with an excuse to explain why it didn't "work out." It really wasn't their fault; blaming someone else for the failure is how the average person copes with the setback.

As a real estate agent, I got my chance to quit once again in 2007. My year started out great. I had sold a house every week through the first six months. I was feeling good, but things suddenly changed. Lenders changed guidelines. Transactions were falling through. Buyers became hesitant. Within a matter of weeks, I felt buried.

Even though I had a great first half of the year, I was still recovering financially from a divorce three years prior; so, when the money stopped coming in, I was drowning in debt. You have heard of trying to keep your head above water. Well, I was so deep in debt that it felt as if I had an anchor tied to my left foot and the only thing above water was the tip of the middle finger on my right hand. However, after momentarily taking a couple punches and falling down, this time I decided not to quit. I knew that I could only fail if I did not get back up. All you have to do is get back up more times than you've fallen and you will end up a success.

I wasn't going to do it on my own this time. I knew I needed help.

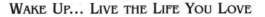

Understand I had been praying and believing things would turn around, but it seemed my prayers were not being answered in the way I wanted them. The prayer of "Please bring me some money, God," wasn't working.

I knew that my greatest success was just around the corner, so I finally changed my prayer. I went to my favorite book—the Bible. I saw what King Solomon asked God for in 1 Kings, Chapter 3. Read the story and you'll see he asked for wisdom. So that's what I asked God for—wisdom.

Sure enough, in a couple of days a friend of mine—having no knowledge of my prayer—brought me a book he thought I should read. It was about King Solomon and the wisdom he taught in the Book of Proverbs. The author of that book suggested that it would be wise to read one chapter of Proverbs a day, each day of the month. There are 31 chapters in Proverbs and I read them.

As soon as I applied what I had read, things began to change in an extraordinary way. I started growing and changing into the person I wanted to be. I learned so many things so rapidly that there is not room enough to list them here.

The big shift came when I asked myself a few tough questions: Why am I here? How can I make difference? What is my purpose? When I read *Think and Grow Rich*, I came up with a purpose. However, what I found is that I was somewhat self-serving. I had realized that by making life about myself first, I was not in a state of abundance. I noticed that Jesus said, "I came so you may have life and have it in all of its abundance" (John 10:10, paraphrased).

I thought, "I say I am a Christian, yet I am making my purpose about me. Maybe that's why I am not experiencing the abundant life Jesus said He had for me." Whatever your faith is, I respect it. I am not here to say you need to believe in God or Jesus. But at the very least, look at the Scriptures I have shared and believe God. Believe in the power of wisdom.

Believe in the abundant life. Picture what life would really be like if you had it in all of its abundance—if you had more wisdom to move forward in. Could you come up with a purpose for your life that is not self-serving?

Here is the purpose that I decided to live by. I say "decided" because I also want you to know that our lives are filled with choices and you get to choose your destiny and your contribution to this world. Here is mine: I glorify God by helping people discover the unstoppable power they have within them.

Whether you know it or not, you already have everything inside you that it takes to be successful and purposeful in life. You have the unstoppable power to create a life you will love. What you need to do if you have not done so is take action. Do something—don't just sit around and talk about it, go do it. Do it in a way that it encourages, strengthens and comforts as many people as you can. Do it today. Don't wait until everything is perfect in your life. Live the life you love right now and the rest will follow.

As I write this, my real estate business is flourishing and I have been transitioning myself into an inspirational speaker and life coach. I am starting with my sphere, and my church, but with a vision to touch as many people in this world as possible. I hope to meet you someday and hear your story of how you got up one more time than you fell, sought wisdom and found your purpose. You are a world changer and a history maker; you are unstoppable.

Go for it!

Chuck Carstensen

FINDING THE TRUE PASSION THAT DRIVES MY LIFE

Maritza Fernandez

How am I living out my dreams and passions in my life? That is the one question I have always asked myself. Searching for the answer has made my quest in life an amazing journey. Throughout my life, my true dreams and passions have manifested themselves in different ways. Coming to this nation as a Cuban immigrant, I have used motherhood and business entrepreneurship as tools to guide and motivate others. All of these elements have one thing in common: They communicate with others the lessons I have learned in order to empower them to achieve their true desires and dreams.

I faced the first challenge in my life at the age of seven, when I traveled from Cuba to an unknown nation. I was afraid, and uncertain of the outcome. I faced a communication barrier, and that was the first time I realized a force exists within each one of us that drives us to succeed and conquer the biggest hurdles. I was able to learn the English language in six months. I also realized the amazing opportunity I had in my new homeland which offered me the freedom to realize my true dreams in life. I have the best of both worlds—two cultures, each one unique. I can be very Cuban, but I can also be as American as apple pie.

My true passion is to communicate with others and to give of myself unconditionally. What better way to fulfill my dreams as the mother of four beautiful children? I was able to send out that message and visualize my desire and passion for motherhood. Life and the universe replied with the greatest reward, my children. The challenge of a mother is to carefully guide her children to develop and fulfill their dreams and passions.

I can remember many times when the subject of careers would come up in discussion with my children, I would always mention that, in life, it is not important what dollar value society places on the choices we make, but it matters where your passion and your drive take you. Making sure my children understood that passion lies in success was my objective.

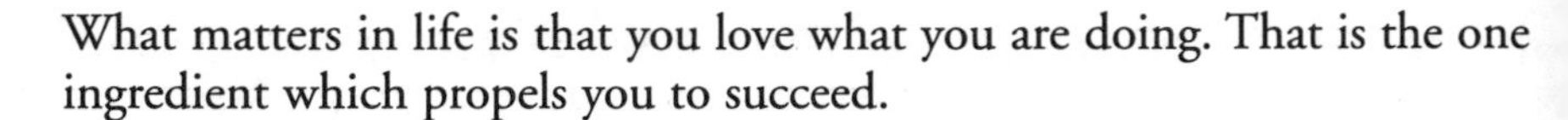

What matters in life is that you love what you are doing. That is the one ingredient which propels you to succeed.

Children are the product of love and a desire to procreate life. It is important to realize when guiding those we love that it is their dreams and passions that lie ahead—not ours. We have children not for ourselves, but for humanity, and that is why their minds and hearts must be guided towards unconditional love.

Business entrepreneurship and self-employment have been my playground for over 30 years. I say "playground" because thinking playfully of work allowed me to savor and enjoy every challenge. I venture to say those challenges that seemed to be impossible but attainable were the most rewarding successes of my life. My motto is, never be afraid to venture into the unknown. My business endeavors have been unique experiences including an automobile repair shop, a car rental company, a warehouse storage facility, a gas station, a fast food restaurant, a mortgage broker company, a multi-family apartment complex, a realty business and a hair salon. These amazing ventures have gifted me with incredible business and have allowed me to know what works for me and what does not. Through all of this, my main focus was to be able to give service without holding back.

There is a valuable point to all this: Never allow yourself to absorb the negative opinions of others which can hold you back and limit what you can achieve. If I would have listened to all the reasons why I could not achieve, I would not be who I am today. The "victim syndrome" was not one of my options. This would not have let me realize my dreams. I can honestly say the limits we have in our lives are set by ourselves.

So, how can any one of us start to realize our potential in life and discover whether or not we are living our dreams? We must always focus as we journey through life. Every turning point in life has its challenges, but we cannot focus on failures. There are no failures—only lessons to be learned. These lessons produce tremendous growth and expansion oppor-

tunities. Never be afraid to try new ventures, for in the unknown, we can receive the greatest rewards. The greatest of dreams have had many ups and downs, but they have given way to amazing results. Think of great achievements such as the telephone, light bulb, the automobile and the airplane. If great minds had given in to negative opinions, what would we have today? My dream is to share all the challenges, lessons and hardships I experienced to help empower others to succeed and achieve their dreams. Persistence and enthusiasm are the elements that help us forge and sculpt our future. We are the Michelangelos of our own David; working steadily will reveal a great work of art. The true essence of who we are can be expressed by helping to motivate others to realize that anything is possible as long as you have a desire to move forward and to give unconditionally to others.

One thing is clear: Every contribution, no matter how small it may seem, can change the world. Negative thoughts can bring more of the same effect. When we realize that each of us is a special link in the chain of life, we are on our way to changing the world. Complete abundance of all our true desires and dreams is the intended state for all humanity.

Maritza Fernandez

LAUGH OFTEN ~ LIVE WELL

Kathy Keaton

When I work, I hear whispers behind my back: "I want her job." It's true. My job is fun. I dispense humor and laughter throughout the halls of local hospitals and nursing homes as a "Humor Therapist." Translation: I'm a clown.

But my job isn't always easy.

Humor therapy is the addition of fun, light-heartedness, laughter or humor in a non-traditional setting. My job as a hospital clown is to present an opportunity for laughter at just the right time, the right place, with the right people. As in life, timing is everything. The real challenge is that those three important components are constantly changing as I push my humor therapy buggy full of music, magic and juggling paraphernalia through the hospital halls. I have to quickly and quietly observe body language, look for eye contact and instantly assess each individual situation as I approach each patient's room. It is a precarious balancing act to connect humor to illness, stress, fear and pain.

So, how did I become a clown? Well, it happened almost overnight. My boys had merrily skipped off to their new school and my husband flew off on a secret military assignment. Alone in a new town, in a new house and stationed at a new military base, I decided I wanted to do something fun that didn't feel like work. My idea: dress up like a clown to help mothers throw parties, play games and cut birthday cake. I had never met a clown or even seen one, except in the circus. The next day when the boys came home from school, I had chosen the name "Piccolo," sewn myself a clown suit and applied my makeup. I was eager and ready. I flashed my huge red smile and waved at passing cars while driving the boys to the ballpark. My nine-year-old was slumped down in the back seat with his ball cap pulled over his face. My five-year-old wanted to know when he could take me to show-and-tell. I was just somebody's mother dressed up to look like a clown. Not a real clown at all.

I remember the exact moment I became a real clown. It happened in an instant while standing on a chair. As the elevator doors opened, I took a deep breath. I was desperate. I had made a promise to a woman I had just met in the elevator on my way to the children's ward with a handful of colorful balloons. My promise was to visit her injured husband, Kenny. At that time I—like many people—believed that clowns were just for kids, and Kenny was definitely an adult.

As I stepped off the elevator, my prayer was short. "Please help me, lead me, guide me and use me." Doubt filled my entire being. *What should I say? What can I do? Is this appropriate? The right time and right place?* My feet wanted to turn and run in the other direction. With my heart beating wildly, I entered the hospital room, pulled the visitor's chair up next to the bed, and suddenly, I stood up on the chair. That was the moment something inside of me changed. With courage and commitment, "Piccolo" began to play *The Marines' Hymn* on her homemade kazoo, complete with bananas, birds, flowers and a kitchen funnel. The mouth of the severely injured marine began to turn up ever so slightly at the corners. As the newborn clown continued to play, Kenny's smile increased and then he began to laugh. His wife started to cry, friends began to applaud and the nurses went for the doctor.

Kenny's laughter and response to the totally absurd, red-headed clown squawking out his beloved patriotic theme song was a much-needed sign that his depression could lift. That spontaneous moment was also a much-needed sign for me—an awakening. It gave me permission to stop listening to the negative words of others and listen to my own heart and intuition. The message was loud and clear: "It is okay to laugh and be joyful—even as a mature adult. Clowns are not just for kids." This was my gift.

Humor is an attitude—the way we look at and perceive the world and what's going on around us. Laughter is the physical response to humor. The physical act of laughing creates positive chemical changes in our brain that affect many parts of our entire body. Even a smile can begin the process. Scientists have discovered that laughter lowers blood pressure, decreases stress and pain, and increases T cells that help our bodies defend against the flu, cold and infection. I believed that was true, but received confirmation once I joined The American Association of Therapeutic Humor.

Today I am one of the compassionate and caring clowns of Clowns of America International and The Texas Clown Association who have made the connection between humor, laughter, harmony and wellness. In many facilities, humor therapy has become a growingly respected resource to help medical professionals treat the entire person—mind, body and soul, as well as the illness. Clowns are now contributing to the well-being of patients, caregivers and professional staff, not only in hospitals, but in other non-traditional settings such as hospices, cancer clinics, rehabilitation centers and Alzheimer's facilities as well.

Experts agree that stress is the underlying cause of many of our illnesses. Laughter yoga, laughter clubs and laughter circles are now becoming popular for groups, businesses and organizations. Organized laughter activities include planned stretching, laughing and breathing exercises. They are a fun and easy way to decrease stress, relax, rejuvenate and connect co-workers and management on a different level.

My passion for knowledge about the healing power of humor has led me to keynote speaking engagements, as well as special appearances at conventions, seminars and workshops. These events mix education and entertainment with the health benefits of humor and laughter. People who could not allow themselves to laugh have shared with me a newfound awareness that they were the ones who needed laughter the most.

When we were children, we laughed freely and spontaneously. For most of us that changes as we get older. But, buried inside each of us, our former child wonders, "What in the heck happened?"

It is my intention in all that I do as a clown not only to share humor and laughter, but also to encourage others to enjoy life, laugh more and recapture the natural joy of childhood. In doing so, I receive the happiness and joy associated with sharing the gift that I've received.

Laughter truly is the best medicine. It's a free, natural resource with no prescription required. By giving yourself permission to laugh harder, longer and more often, you can encourage others to do the same. By sharing humor with others, you not only decrease your own stress, but have a positive effect on the atmosphere and the attitude of those around you. I encourage you to laugh more—laugh often and live well.

Kathy Keaton

WAKE UP!

Steven E

All the signs were there. They had always been there, waiting to be read. Waiting to show the way to prosperity, freedom, peace and fulfillment.

But I was too busy trying to succeed to read the signs. I was in such a hurry that I didn't have time to stop, not to ask for directions, not to look around at where I was and where I was going. I didn't even have time to stop to put gas in the tank. If that sounds familiar, then this could be an important story for you.

I cannot tell you what made me slow down and read the signs, but it was probably the collective weight of failures and disappointments. It was the friction created by rubbing your friends and family the wrong way, or the inertia of bouncing off stone walls. Perhaps, it was all those things and more. Whatever it was, one day I stopped long enough to hear a small voice that asked, "Is this really what you want?"

Of course, it wasn't.

So, I took some of the advice that I had received from my mom, years before. It was the same advice I had been giving to people with whom I worked as a professional trainer. "Get up!" I said to myself. "Decide what you want to do, focus on it, and get going. Don't quit until you have it; don't even consider quitting until you have it. Get up!"

I will spare you the details, but it worked. As if by magic, I seemed to get more done during the same period of time. I was happier, felt more fulfilled, and seemed to be more popular and well received by others. It seemed to me that I had only to "Get up!" and my life changed. I decided to write a book about this phenomenon.

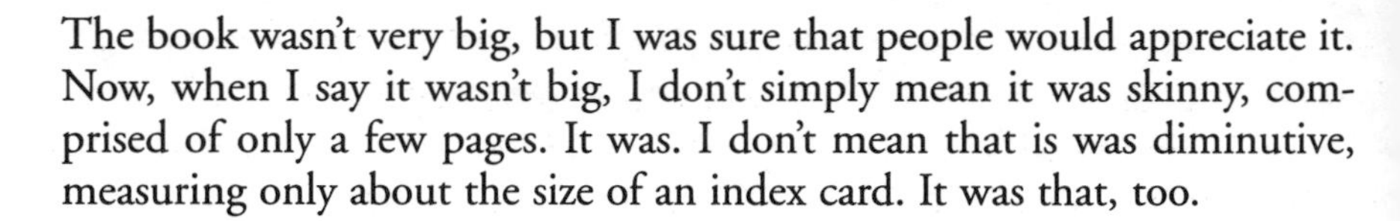

The book wasn't very big, but I was sure that people would appreciate it. Now, when I say it wasn't big, I don't simply mean it was skinny, comprised of only a few pages. It was. I don't mean that is was diminutive, measuring only about the size of an index card. It was that, too.

It was also "not very big" in the bookstores. I had called it, "Wake Up!" but no one seemed to be very awake around that book. I was disappointed.

I could have gone back to my "busy going nowhere" lifestyle. However, I had been blessed by some insights that gave new meaning to my new mantra. I had seen myself as a writer, helping dozens—perhaps even hundreds or thousands of people—to "Wake Up!" The vision was as clear as a motion picture, as vivid as a favorite memory. I could not make it go away, and I certainly did not want to do so. I decided to write another book and to improve my effort with what I had learned.

I recruited several of my friends to write inspirational chapters, lessons or poems. I scrambled for months until my book was assembled. It was printed and sold. Today, I am working on the thirtieth such book in the series. The motion picture, you see, had a sequel. I had visualized my future and it came to be.

Here is a good example of how to visualize from *Wake Up*. I visualized myself living on one of the most beautiful beaches in the world each morning and at bedtime for six months. Long before I moved there I clearly visualized myself sitting, looking out over Victoria Beach, seeing and hearing the ocean waves crashing on the California shore. I felt the ocean breeze on my face; I smelled the salty sea air.

The most important part of visualization is to make sure you feel it. Plant the seeds and know that, someday, your seeds will become beautiful flowers. Just wait, let go and trust. There is no reason to transplant the seeds just because you don't see instant growth. Make sure you water them daily and have faith.

Practice this visualization with your relationships. See yourself with more unconditional love, joy, compassion and everything your heart desires. Do this: Write down three things you would like to manifest into your life. Carry these goals in your pocket throughout the day, concentrating on them. Feel them being in your life. Feel that they exist in the present moment, in the now. The more you observe and concentrate on your goals, the faster they will come to you.

So many people have faith in the dreams of others. They trust in futures outlined by strangers. They will probably be disappointed. Trust in yourself as you visualize your own life that will surely be. It's what happens when you finally decide to wake up and live the life you love.

Steven E

AUTHOR INDEX

Bank, Laura Ph.D., PA-C ***7***

Dr. Laura Bank's successful career in teaching and administration has naturally progressed into writing and speaking. Currently Laura is the associate program director at A.T. Still University's Physician Assistant Program. Her body-mind-spirit philosophy joyfully affects everyone around her as she helps people move towards a state of optimal health and wellness. Please visit Laura's Web site for a free sample of her first book, *Pearls of Wellness*, at PearlsOfWellnessBook.com.

Web site: www.PearlsOfWellnessBook.com
E-mail: BankOnYourHealth@gmail.com

Beard, Lee ***1***

Lee is a television producer, advertising executive and business developer. He lives in Arkansas when not traveling as the co-creator of the *Wake Up...Live the Life You Love* book series. Lee is an author featured in more than a dozen motivational and inspirational volumes. He concentrates on bringing the power of the Wake Up network to bear on the challenges of business development. If you've had a "wake up" moment you would like to share, visit wakeupmoment.com to tell your story!

Web site: www.wakeupmoment.com, www.wakeuplive.net, leebeard.com
E-mail: lee@wakeuplive.net

Beiler, Susie ***141***

Susie is a certified holistic health counselor and occupational therapist. Her services include comprehensive personalized health assessments, private counseling sessions, workshops, group programs, speaking engagements, Raindrop Technique with essential oils, health food store tours and corporate wellness programs. She is creating a healing sanctuary in Pennsylvania. Her holistic nutrition DVDs are for sale on her Web site.

Address: 1210 Old York Road, Suite 202
Warminster, PA 18974
Telephone: 267-307-4224
Web sites: susie.younglivingworld.com, susiebeiler.blogspot.com

Bickert, Dr. John G. ***93***

Dr. John Bickert is a chiropractor in Southeast Calgary, Alberta. He and his wife, Gail, have five children. He has practiced chiropractic medicine for more than 20 years and has spent a similar amount of time as a high school science teacher in Edmonton and Calgary. Dr. Bickert acts as a consultant to various business groups and non-profit corporations internationally and is CEO of Lapanto Group International, Inc.

Web site: www.lgii.net
E-mail: author@lgii.net

CEO of Terri's Consign & Design Franchise Co., Terri is a leader in sustainable business practices with a long history and passion for keeping our planet green. For nearly 30 years, Terri has grown a multi-million dollar chain of consignment stores and franchises coast to coast. Terri's personal and professional success story is one of inspiration and motivation, and she is recipient of over 30 national awards. Entrepreneur, author and renowned speaker, Terri has been seen on Oprah, CNN and CNBC's Big Idea.

Address: 1375 W. Drivers Way
Tempe, AZ 85284
Telephone: 480-969-1121
E-mail: terri@eterris.com

Chuck is a father of two wonderful kids, Chloe and Chase. He is a Real Estate agent with RE/MAX Associates Plus, Elk River, MN. He is passionate about his faith and believes the marketplace is a great spot to be a minister. Chuck is passionate about personal development and is an affiliate with an excellent company and business opportunity—Success University. His true passion is as an inspirational and motivational speaker and life coach and is transitioning into a career in that field.

Telephone: 612-290-3809
Web sites: www.chuckcarstensen.com, www.DiscoverYourSuccess.net
E-mail: chuck@thediscoveryteam.com

Phil Conway represents the fourth generation of the Conway family, along with his brother Kevin, serving the Greater Peabody and the North Shore of Boston, MA, for 114 years. He served as Past President of Massachusetts Funeral Directors Associates and as Policy Board for the National Funeral Directors Association. He has also held leadership positions with the Massachusetts Junior Chamber of Commerce and the Jaycees.

Address: P.O. Box 3063
Peabody, MA 01960
E-mail: binspired@gmail.com

Best-selling author and lecturer.

Wayne is the author of these best-selling books: *Power of Intention, Real Magic, Manifesting Your Destiny* and *Pulling Your Own Strings.*

Born in Havana Cuba, Maritza immigrated to the United States in 1967 and began her amazing journey. She is the mother of four children and is a successful business owner, entrepreneur, investor and developer.

E-mail: PumpGo@bellsouth.net

Gallapoo, Daniel *15*

Daniel Gallapoo, "Doberman Dan," is a direct response marketing consultant and copywriter. His specialty is helping clients double and triple their sales using a combination of online and offline marketing.

Address: 3512 E Silver Springs Blvd. Suite 119
Ocala, FL 34470
Telephone: 813-413-4057
Web site: www.dobermandan.com

Gilbert, Rayeleen *67*

Rayeleen Gilbert is a Clinical Hypnotherapist & EFT Practitioner. Rayeleen is deeply committed to the evolution of consciousness and guiding others to true self-acceptance and self-love. She lives the life she loves with her beloved husband, Jeffrey, three children, Raymond, Ashlie and Shatika and three step-children, Travis, Zacary and Carly.

Address: P.O. Box 3803
Success, WA 6964
Telephone: +61423335848
Web site: www.yes2life.com.au
E-mail: rayeleen@yes2life.com.au

Graham, Simon *113*

Simon resides in Sydney, Australia overlooking beautiful Sydney Harbour. When not sailing or enjoying the local beaches he runs the innovative Insiders Reveal book brand, enabling senior experienced people to pass on their inside career knowledge to the next generation. Simon can be contacted at www.insidersreveal.com

Web site: www.insidersreveal.com
E-mail: Visit Web site

Henderson, R. Winn, M.D. *99*

Dr. R. Winn Henderson, #1 best-selling author, has written or co-written 33 books. He also hosts the internationally syndicated radio talk show Share Your Mission. If you have a mission and a passion you want to pursue, there is no better platform than a radio internet talk show in which to share it with the world. He can teach you how to get on the air and broadcasting in 30 days or less.

Telephone: 877-787-3127 (toll free)
Web sites: www.theultimatesecrettohappiness.com, www.winnhendersonmd.freelife.com
E-mail: drhenderson7@mchsi.com

Hinson, David R. *63*

David R. Hinson is an entrepreneur in the computer, personal development and real estate industries. David is a speaker, mentor and advisor to businesses and professionals throughout the nation. He has over twenty years of public service to his country and community.

Dreams Realized, LLC
Address: P.O. Box 77032
Washington, DC 20002
Web sites: www.davidhinson.com, www.kwik-ez-homebuyer.com

Holdmann, Jan *137*

Jan is an author, motivational speaker, former Toastmaster and director of the Janus Advocate Team. She conducts numerous business, spiritual and self-image improvement workshops. She is also an SRT practitioner and psycho-spiritual therapist. For information on appointments, upcoming events or to receive her free, weekly motivational newsletter please go to www.janusteam.com.

Address: 1300S. Watson Rd, #A114, PMB #214
Buckeye, AZ 85326
Telephone: 877-392-0668
E-mail: jholdmann@janusteam.com

Hudson, Ernie *3*

Ernie is currently acting and writing for TV and film and is available for speaking and personal appearances. Ernie has performed in various TV shows, movies and plays, including *Taxi, OZ, Ghost Busters, The Hand that Rocks the Cradle, Congo, Miss Congeniality, The Crow* and a variety of others. He has also written two published plays, *Rebellion 369* and *My Kingdom Come*, and is working on others in the near future. His personal representative, Thomas Cushing, can be contacted at Innovative Artist, 310-656-0400, and Ernie can be reached through his Web site.

Web site: www.Ernie-Hudson.com.

Jacobs, John R. *11*

John Jacobs is founder and president of Healthier Living 4 You, a company dedicated to bringing advanced medical products and nutraceutical supplements to people around the world. John based his life and business around the teachings of Dr. Wayne Dyer and others who espouse living in harmony with the world and by giving back as much as we can. Healthier Living 4 You carries this tradition through its advanced healthcare technology and education seminars to dramatically change people's health and happiness.

Address: Healthier Living 4 You
Wellesley, Ont. Canada NoB2T0
Web site: www.HL4Y.com
E-mail: john@HL4Y.com

Jenkin, Billie Willmon 109

As a teacher, Billie Willmon Jenkin saw a need for emotional education of both teachers and students. Before retirement, she developed and facilitated a course in attitude change for adult prison inmates. Her passion for empowering others to make positive changes in their lives is evident in her writing, mentoring and speaking. *The Knock-Kneed Cowboy*, her first children's book, which she wrote and illustrated, is a joyful, empowering tale of individuality.

Telephone: 832-285-8037
Web site: www.EmpoweringForChange.com
E-mail: Billie@EmpoweringForChange.com

Keaton, Kathy ***153***

Kathy Keaton (Piccolo the Clown) is a keynote speaker and clown of 30 years. She established the first Hospital Humor Therapy Program in West Texas. Kathy, as "Piccolo," delivers her educational message via laughing circles while interjecting the healthy benefits of humor and laughter in a fun and memorable way. She has directed and co-produced a hospice grief DVD for children and families called "Clowns Cry Too"

Telephone: 325-944-4746
Web site: www.piccolotheclown.com
Email: kpiccolo28@juno.co

Kimes, Dr. Heavenly ***107***

Dr. Kimes is a graduate of Florida A&M University and Meharry Medical College. She is happily married to Dr. Damon Kimes. She has spent years educating herself on wealth building and is on a crusade to educate professional and business owners on her proven wealth building techniques.

Address: 1810 GA Hwy. 20 Ste 172
Conyers, GA 30013
Telephone: 404-713-4982
Web site: www.heavenlykimes.com

Lacey, Ed ***19***

Ed Lacey was commissioned in 1978 after graduating from the University of Alabama. He retired from the Army in 1995 as a Major in the Special Forces. He is married to the former Kathleen M. Parent and they reside in Bartlett, Illinois. Currently, Major Lacey is President and CEO of Synergy Financial Solutions, Inc. He is a graduate of the UIC Network Marketing certification course and Anthony Robbins Mastery University. He was voted Business member of 2003 from the Bartlett Chamber of Commerce.

Telephone: 630-736-0388, Toll free: 877-234-9793
Web site: www.edlaceyjr.com
E-mail: ed@edlaceyjr.com

Levi, Zachary ***39***

At the early age of six, Zachary began acting, singing and dancing in school and local theater productions. He has performed in regional roles such as *Grease, The Outsiders, Oliver, The Wizard of Oz* and *Big River*. But, it was his portrayal of Jesus in Ojai's *Godspell* that brought him to the attention of Hollywood. He completed a supporting role in the television movie *Big Shot: Confessions of a Campus Bookie* (2002) (TV). He then began acting as Kipp Steadman in the TV series *Less Than Perfect* (2002) and was also seen in the television movie (2003) (TV) on the WB. He also stars in NBC's *Chuck*. In his spare time, Zachary enjoys skateboarding, snowboarding, skydiving and participating in various other sports (Bio information obtained from www.IMDB.com).

Lizer, Dr. Gerald W. *49*

Dr. Gerald Lizer has been in private practice for more than 30 years. He has traveled the world and studied health care in many nations. Lizer was one of the first doctors to research using lasers to heal the body instead of cutting. He writes for a local paper and has patients who have come to his office from several other states and speaks to groups on a regular basis on several topics related to enhancing our health and wellness. Dr. Lizer always tries to be on the cutting edge of technology.

Address: P.O. Box 709
Eagle River, AK 99577
Telephone: 907-694-9535
E-mail: Drlizer@alaska.net

McGinty, Timothy A. *117*

Mr. Timothy A. McGinty is founder and president of Imagine Yourself.... Imagine Yourself... assists individuals and organizations in closing the gap between their potential and performance so they achieve their goals faster and ultimately enjoy life more! How blissful is your life?

Imagine Yourself
Address: 13477 Prospect Rd. Suite 204
Strongsville, OH 44149
Telephone: 440-236-6519
Web site: www.timothymcginty.com
E-mail: tim@timothymcginty.com

Meierhoefer, Axel *89*

Axel is a coach, trainer, teacher, consultant, speaker, and soon to be doctor with a Ph.D. in leadership. He has years of international experience in helping companies, large and small, as well as individuals find ways to improve themselves, their performance and discover their potential and enjoy life. By applying a proven system and the Universal Tape Measure of Human Performance anyone can discover their personal Performance profile and improve in weeks rather than years.

Address: 420 Dogwood Drive
Buellton, CA 93427
Web site: www.ecoconsciouspioneers.com
E-mail: AM@Meierhoefer.net

Nair, Ashok P. *31*

Ashok Nair lives in Abbotsford, British Columbia with his wife and six-year-old son. He works as a consultant and teacher helping men and women who want to get connected with their real self and lead a blissful life. As a Healer, Speaker & Happiness Consultant, he assists individuals to create new realm of possibilities in their lives.

Certified Business Coach
Address: 31130 Southern Dr.
Abbotsford, BC V2T 5K2
Telephone: 604-614-8733
Web sites: www.MessagesFromMymasters.com, www.omnificSuccessStrategies.com
E-mail: ashokvell@gmail.com

Author and Speaker: Embracing personal transformation in the adventure of awakening. Len Z. Nichols has been involved in the field of human development for the past 28 years as a Psychiatric Nurse, Master Social Worker, Hypnotist, Marital/Family Therapist and university educator. He has facilitated workshops in both the United States and Canada is the author of *Saving the Planet from Ourselves: Our Awakening is Just Around the Bend.*

Telephone: 325-944-9996
Web site: www.lenznichols.com
E-mail: nicholsawakening@msn.com

As a spiritual teacher and guide, Patrick O'Connor has devoted his life to integrating and deepening his own spiritual transformation in order to guide others with theirs. Born in the U.S., Patrick is currently traveling the world offering coaching, workshops and retreats; utilizing fasting as a catalyst to assist in creating individual awakenings and healings. He has also released an e-book, Journey to Nourish the Soul, which chronicles his adventures and lessons, learned during a 7-month solo backpacking adventure throughout Southeast Asia as a "U.S. Ambassador of Love."

Telephone: 407-278-5761
Web site: www.thefastingpath.com
E-mail: patrick@thefastingpath.com

Joanne Rainey lives in Phoenix, Arizona with her husband and two boys. She owns a business consulting firm and is a frequent speaker for industry trade associations. She has been a featured columnist in the Phoenix Business Journal and her articles have been published internationally. Joanne is currently working on a book about finding your personal key to success.

Address: 7939 West Sands Drive
Peoria, AZ 85383
Telephone: 623-203-2136
Web site: www.findingyourkeytosuccess.com
Email: joanne.rainey@findingyourkeytosuccess.com

Conrad Raw is a speaker, author and trainer committed to bringing people the most effective courses and seminars for personal and spiritual growth with an emphasis on practical application. He travels the world to learn and has a passion for teaching people how to activate the hidden powers of their mind using cutting edge teaching strategies. He is the author of *The Forbidden Secrets of Personal and Energetic Development*. Through his free newsletter he provides coaching, insights and information to help people activate a higher level of conciousness.

Web site: www.GreaterHumanPotentials.com
E-mail: info@greaterhumanpotential.com

A #1 best-selling author, Gregory Scott Reid has become known for his energy and candor on the speaker's platform and his signature phrase "Always Good!" An experienced entrepreneur in his own right, he has become known as an effective leader, coach and "The Millionaire Mentor."

Website: www.AlwaysGood.com

Rodriguez, Raul G. M.D. *25*

Dr. Rodriguez is a Colombian psychiatrist specializing in chemical dependency and the management of chronic pain. He currently works at a private psychiatric hospital in the heart of Texas. His mission is to help anyone with whom he has contact with, and to help them to realize his/her inner potential and reach abundance, inner peace and happiness without sorrow.

Address: P.O. Box 60618
San Angelo, Texas 76906-0618

Silverman, Aaron *85*

Aaron Silverman is a Real Estate Investor and creator of Money Smarts Management Personal Financial Ezine and Education. He achieved his M.S. in Environmental Resources Management from the Florida Institute of Technology, and his B.S. in Biology at Newberry College.

Address: 164 Market St. #123,
Charleston, SC 29401
Web site: www.aaronsilverman.com
Email: aaron@aaronsilverman.com

Simms, Ena M. *121*

Author of the inspirational poetry book, *Look Up and be Lifted Up*. Ena believes that anyone can accomplish anything if they really want to. Writing is one of the passions she acquired at a very young age. She took writing seriously after she realized the soul-changing effect it had. She wants to financially position herself to be able to help troubled youths in Canada and ultimately all over the world.

Address: Toronto, Canada
E-mail: enasimms@rogers.com

Stetson, Jon *41*

Jon Stetson is the one entertainer/speaker in America who truly understands the meaning and importance of capturing the minds and hearts of an audience. Jon has had many television appearances and has performed in 23 countries. He has been invited to the White House on five occasions.

The Stetson Experience
Web site: www.jonstetson.com
E-mail: jon@jonstetson.com

Steven E *157*

Creator of *Wake Up...Live the Life You Love*. With more than 12 million stories in print, his message is inspiring an international audience. Steven E has been joined in the book series by such noted speakers as Dr. Wayne Dyer, Brian Tracy, John Assaraf, and many more inspirational souls. He is now coaching select individuals on the development of a multimillion dollar information business with their own message to inspire people around the world.

Web sites: stevene.com and wakeupstore.com/pcc

Strong, Judy *71*

Judy Strong is an author and speaker who shares her passion for personal growth and life-building. Through writing and connecting with people, Judy gives others the tools to handle adversity and move forward with confidence and a sense of direction.

Address: 2550 S. Ellsworth Rd. #758
Mesa, AZ 85209
Telephone: 480-219-7785
Web site: www.notimetogrieve.com
E-mail: judystrong758@hotmail.com

Tracy, Brian *75*

Brian Tracy is the most listened to audio author on personal and business success in the world today. His fast-moving talks and seminars on leadership, sales, managerial effectiveness and business strategy are loaded with powerful, proven ideas and strategies that people can immediately apply to get better results in every area.

Brian Tracy International
Address: 462 Stevens Ave., Suite 202
Solana Beach, CA 92075
Telephone: 858-436-7300
Web site: www.BrianTracy.com
E-mail: BrianTracy@briantracy.com

Tuscani, Giorgio 55

Giorgio Tuscani had been producing private commissioned art until 2007. That summer, Mr. Tuscani held his first public art exhibit titled "The Endless Dance Of Souls That Become One...The Soul of My Art," which was a huge success. With over three hundred people attending the sold-out show, Mr. Tuscani couldn't have been more grateful and appreciative. Mr. Tuscani is known by all as "The Artist of the Soul."

Telephone: 818-754-1178, 310-779-4297
Web site: www.giorgiotuscaniart.com

Vassey, Liz *135*

Liz began acting at the age of nine (portraying Oliver in the musical of the same name) and continued to work extensively on the stage, performing in over fifty plays at regional and professional theaters in the Tampa Bay area. Liz has appeared as a regular or recurring character on nine television shows including *CSI, The Tick, Maximum Bob, Brotherly Love* and *All My Children* (for which she was nominated for a Daytime Emmy). Her hobbies are writing (she has sold two potential pilot scripts to studios), scuba diving and running (Bio information obtained from www.IMBD.com).

Viard, Dominique (Nicky) *29*

Nicky Viard worked for 11 years as the purchasing director for the owner of a major shopping center. She is now an aspiring writer and lives in New York. She loves dogs and enjoys exercising, bike riding and reading.

E-mail: dviard220@yahoo.com

Williams, Cutressa M. *45*

Cutressa is the CEO of Abundant Success Institute and Consulting LLC, and an author, speaker, radio host, law student, real estate mogul and future governor of Alabama (2022). Cutressa is the proud parent of Aspen Alece Moniquee and her future adopted girls from around the world.

Address: 3325 Lorna Rd. #2-110
Birmingham, AL 35216
Telephone: 205-945-6066 Fax: 740-931-3324
Web site: www.cutressamwilliams.com
E-mail: cutressawilliams@gmail.com

Wilson, Sabrina-Marie *81*

Sabrina-Marie Wilson is President & CEO of HEART, Inc., a non-profit organization that promotes excellence and life success principles to "people of different abilities." Author, consultant and media strategist for national organizations that promote quality healthcare and civil rights. Sabrina-Marie is a recipient of numerous national honorsShe has appeared on television, national radio, in beauty, health and fitness magazines, and before the Congressional Black Caucus' Annual Legislative Braintrust.

Web site: Sabrina-MarieWilson.com
E-mail: Sabrina-Marie@sabrina-mariewilson.com, info@sabrinamariewilson.com

Wake Up...
Live the Life You Love

Wake Up Moments

Resources

RESOURCES

The Wealth Creator Source
1-888-504-6257
www.WealthCreatorSource.com

The Wealth Creator Source is the Internet's premier place to acquire expert advice on investing, real estate, personal success, starting your business and much more. Members of the Wealth Creator Source have access to over 90 interviews with some of the greatest wealth experts and entrepreneurs on the planet. When you join you'll receive a new CD interview with another leading wealth expert every month.

The list includes experts such as: Robert Kiyosaki (*Rich Dad, Poor Dad*), Stephen R. Covey (*The Speed of Trust*), Jack Canfield (co-creator *Chicken Soup for the Soul*), T. Harv Eker (*The Millionaire Mind*) and Brian Tracy.

When you listen to a Wealth Creator Source interview you'll receive advice that you won't find anywhere else, you'll get information and proven techniques you can use right away to drive more income into your pocket.

"The smartest thing you can ever do is to admire successful people, emulate them, look up to them, read their books, listen to their tapes, go to their courses, study their notes, talk to them whenever you can."—Brian Tracy, world famous entrepreneur.

Get access to all the interviews for 30 days for only $1.00. Sign up for your trial membership now! Go to: www.WealthCreatorSource.com

RESOURCES

Early To Rise
866-344-7200
www.EarlyToRise.com

Early To Rise is the Internet's most popular health, wealth and success e-zine. Their purpose is to support their readers in a quest to succeed in life. When you sign up for Early To Rise, you will receive a message in your e-mail inbox every morning, full of good cheer and useful advice; you will be armed with loads of experience, useful insights and great resources.

Early To Rise wants you to succeed in any area of life you wish. They can give you inspiration or show you how it's done. Their goal is to get you to understand something, remember something, realize something and, ultimately, to do something that will make you healthier, wealthier and even wiser every day of the year.

When you read Early To Rise, you will be reminded of all that is possible for you. A better, brighter, fuller, and happier future is at your fingertips. Go to www.EarlyToRise.com to sign up for this free e-zine!

Resources

Debbie Allen, CSP
Allen & Associates Consulting, Inc.
PO Box 27946
Scottsdale, AZ 85255-0149
Telephone: 800-359-4544 or 480-634-7691
Fax: 480-634-7692
E-mail: Debbie@DebbieAllen.com
Business Resources: www.SalesandMarketingSuccess.com
Video BLOG: www.ShamelessDiva.com

Debbie Allen has built and sold several highly-successful companies in a diverse range of industries. She now teaches others the secrets of success with her insightful business-building strategies. Her contagious enthusiasm inspires others to move past the limiting beliefs that hold them back from their peak potentials in business and life.

As a 12-year international business speaker, Debbie Allen has presented before thousands of people in 13 countries. She has been named CSP, Certified Speaking Professional, by the National Speakers Association and International Speakers Federation, an honor achieved by less than 10 percent of speakers worldwide. Debbie was also honored by the National Chamber of Commerce with the prestigious Blue Chip Enterprise Award for overcoming obstacles and fast business growth.

Debbie has authored five books on business and personal development including the best-selling book, *Confessions of Shameless Self Promoters.* Her expertise has been featured in dozens of publications including, *Entrepreneur* and *Sales & Marketing Excellence.* She is also a featured expert in four motivational movies including, *The Opus, Pass it On* and *The Compass.*

As a marketing consultant, she can help you grow your business quickly with innovative, low-cost, proven marketing strategies.

Sign up for Debbie's business building e-course and audio download "57 Tips for Attracting Customers Like Crazy" ($100 value for free) at www.SalesandMarketingSuccess.com.

Wake Up...
Live the Life You Love

Wake Up Moments

Noetic Pyramid

Noetic Pyramid

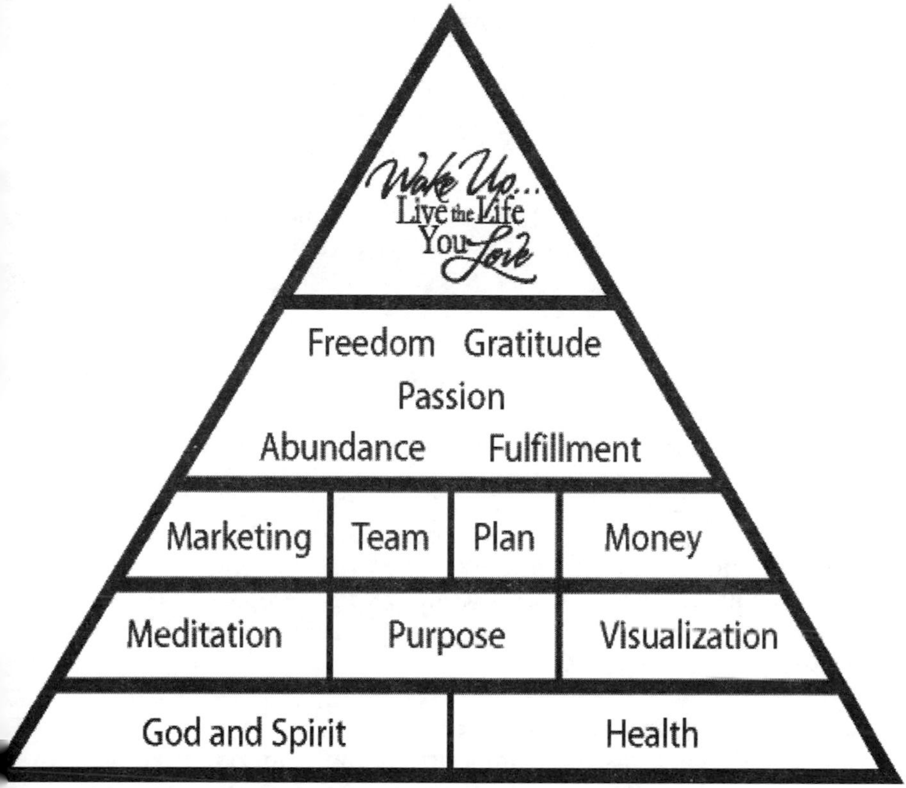

Wake Up... Live the Life You Love

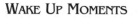

Freedom Gratitude
Passion
Abundance Fulfillment

Marketing | Team | Plan | Money

Meditation | Purpose | Visualization

God and Spirit | Health

The Noetic (no-EH-tik) Pyramid is a systemic way of looking at the benefits of learning and implementing the attitudes, beliefs and behaviors that must always precede real abundance in life.

NOESIS (no-ë´-sis, noun) [Greek. To perceive] 1. Philosophical: Purely intellectual apprehension. 2. Psychological: Cognition, especially through direct and self-evident knowledge. Noetic (adjective).

There is a way to know; therefore, there is a way to know what to do in life. The answers are not concealed from us, but are available through noesis: a purely intellectual process which gives us sure answers, if only we will look and grasp what we see.

But no one can see—or even look with energy and purpose—unless the mind is clear and the attention is directed. We need a guiding principle that gives us a direction and a foundation.

Building on what they have discovered over years of working with teachers, mentors, motivators, philosophers, psychologists and business leaders, Steven E and Lee Beard have devised the Noetic Pyramid: a structure of beliefs and learning that takes us from the firmest of foundations to the kind of life we can most enjoy; the kind of life which can most benefit those around us; the kind of life that may change the world.

Foundations

With your firm faith in God, you have the proper perspective to process all instructions that you receive. Then, when you give adequate attention to your health, you have a solid foundation to allow you to learn and utilize what we call The 7 Secrets of Living the Life You Love.

Charting the Course

Then we must develop the internal structures of abundance: find your purpose through meditation or prayer, then visualize your desired future. To embark on this process without a firm grounding in belief and without the physical tools to support your mind and spirit, you are almost sure to be disappointed.

Reach Out to Expand the Possibilities

The Pyramid then leads you from a firm foundation to the external techniques of planning, teamwork, marketing and acquiring the necessary money. None of these external elements will be meaningful without the foundational elements, but neither will these essential elements inherently lead to abundance.

Abundance and Gratitude
We must realize the benefits of learning and utilize the internal structure and external techniques to create abundance, freedom, gratitude and fulfillment so we can truly live the life we love. An abundant life has meaning beyond ourselves, so we must seek to improve the lives of others. When we use our freedom to the benefit of others, when we are thankful for the opportunity to share the blessings of a materially abundant life, then we are fulfilled beyond our ability to imagine.

This is what we want everyone around the world to do: *Wake Up...Live the Life You Love.*

Wake Up...
Live the Life You Love

Wake Up Moments

A Gift For You

Wake Up...Live the Life You Love wants to give you a gift that will get you moving on the path to personal abundance. Please visit www.wakeupgift.com today!

Notes And Personal Reflections

Notes And Personal Reflections

Notes And Personal Reflections